Charles Lindbergh

*These and other titles are included in The
Importance Of biography series:*

Maya Angelou
Louis Armstrong
James Baldwin
Lucille Ball
The Beatles
Alexander Graham Bell
Napoleon Bonaparte
Julius Caesar
Rachel Carson
Charlie Chaplin
Charlemagne
Winston Churchill
Christopher Columbus
Leonardo da Vinci
James Dean
Charles Dickens
Walt Disney
Dr. Seuss
F. Scott Fitzgerald
Anne Frank
Benjamin Franklin
Mohandas Gandhi
John Glenn
Jane Goodall
Martha Graham
Lorraine Hansberry
Stephen Hawking
Ernest Hemingway
Adolf Hitler

Harry Houdini
Thomas Jefferson
Mother Jones
John F. Kennedy
Martin Luther King Jr.
Bruce Lee
John Lennon
Abraham Lincoln
Joe Louis
Douglas MacArthur
Thurgood Marshall
Margaret Mead
Golda Meir
Mother Teresa
Muhammad
John Muir
Richard M. Nixon
Pablo Picasso
Edgar Allan Poe
Elvis Presley
Queen Elizabeth I
Queen Victoria
Jonas Salk
Margaret Sanger
William Shakespeare
Frank Sinatra
Tecumseh
Simon Wiesenthal

THE IMPORTANCE OF

Charles Lindbergh

by Andy Koopmans

LUCENT
BOOKS®

THOMSON
—✦— ™
GALE

San Diego • Detroit • New York • San Francisco • Cleveland • New Haven, Conn. • Waterville, Maine • London • Munich

On Cover: Charles Lindbergh works on his plane in 1927.

LIBRARY OF CONGRESS CATALOGING-IN-PUBLICATION DATA

Koopmans, Andy.
  Charles Lindbergh / by Andy Koopmans.
    p. cm. — (Importance of)
Includes bibliographical references and index.
Summary: Profiles the childhood, education, interest in aviation, fame, tragedy,
and controversy surrounding the first man to fly solo across the Atlantic Ocean.
  ISBN 1-59018-245-6 (hardback : alk. paper)
  1. Lindbergh, Charles (Charles Augustus), 1902–1974—Juvenile literature.
2. Air pilots—United States—Biography—Juvenile literature. [1. Lindbergh, Charles
(Charles Augustus), 1902–1974. 2. Air pilots.] I. Title. II. Series.
  TL540.L5 K66 2003
  629.13'092—dc21
                                                              2002009882

Printed in the United States of America

Contents

Foreword

THE IMPORTANCE OF biography series deals with individuals who have made a unique contribution to history. The editors of the series have deliberately chosen to cast a wide net and include people from all fields of endeavor. Individuals from politics, music, art, literature, philosophy, science, sports, and religion are all represented. In addition, the editors did not restrict the series to individuals whose accomplishments have helped change the course of history. Of necessity, this criterion would have eliminated many whose contribution was great, though limited. Charles Darwin, for example, was responsible for radically altering the scientific view of the natural history of the world. His achievements continue to impact the study of science today. Others, such as Chief Joseph of the Nez Percé, played a pivotal role in the history of their own people. While Joseph's influence does not extend much beyond the Nez Percé, his nonviolent resistance to white expansion and his continuing role in protecting his tribe and his homeland remain an inspiration to all.

These biographies are more than factual chronicles. Each volume attempts to emphasize an individual's contributions both in his or her own time and for posterity. For example, the voyages of Christopher Columbus opened the way to European colonization of the New World. Unquestionably, his encounter with the New World brought monumental changes to both Europe and the Americas in his day. Today, however, the broader impact of Columbus's voyages is being critically scrutinized. *Christopher Columbus*, as well as every biography in The Importance Of series, includes and evaluates the most recent scholarship available on each subject.

Each author includes a wide variety of primary and secondary source quotations to document and substantiate his or her work. All quotes are footnoted to show readers exactly how and where biographers derive their information, as well as provide stepping stones to further research. These quotations enliven the text by giving readers eyewitness views of the life and times of each individual covered in The Importance Of series.

Finally, each volume is enhanced by photographs, bibliographies, chronologies, and comprehensive indexes. For both the casual reader and the student engaged in research, The Importance Of biographies will be a fascinating adventure into the lives of people who have helped shape humanity's past and present, and who will continue to shape its future.

IMPORTANT DATES IN THE LIFE OF CHARLES LINDBERGH

1902
Lindbergh born on February 4 in Detroit, Michigan.

1922
Drops out of college to become a flying student at Nebraska Standard Aircraft Corporation; makes his first flight on April 9.

1912
Attends his first air meet in Virginia.

1924
Enlists in U.S. Army as a flying cadet.

1926
Makes first Chicago–St. Louis airmail flight.

1929
Marries Anne Morrow Lindbergh.

1905   **1915**   **1925**   **1935**

1920
Enrolls in University of Wisconsin as an engineering student.

1925
Graduates from U.S. Air Service Flying School and is commissioned second lieutenant in Air Service Reserve Corps; becomes chief pilot at Robertson Aircraft in St. Louis.

1932
Son, Charles Lindbergh Jr., kidnapped and killed.

1935
Moves to England with family.

1927
Establishes transcontinental air record, San Diego to New York on May 10–12; flies from New York to Paris, wins Orteig Prize for first nonstop transatlantic flight between the two cities; tours the United States with the *Spirit of St. Louis*; makes first nonstop flight from Washington to Mexico City.

1939
Returns to United States
and begins speaking
against U.S. intervention
in World War II.

1966
Serves until 1972
on World Wildlife
Board of Trustees.

1954
Appointed rank of
brigadier general;
awarded Pulitzer
Prize for the *Spirit
of St. Louis.*

| 1940 | 1950 | 1960 | 1970 |

1942
Works until 1943 as test pilot
and aviation consultant as
part of civilian war effort in
World War II.

1974
Dies from lymphoma on
Maui, Hawaii, on August 26.

1936
Makes first of five
trips to Germany to
evaluate *Luftwaffe.*

The Lindbergh Phenomenon

Aviation was in its infancy on May 20, 1927, when Charles Lindbergh, a twenty-five-year-old airmail pilot from Minnesota, waited aboard his plane, the *Spirit of St. Louis*, on the runway at New York's Roosevelt Field. Lindbergh was a pioneer. He waited to take off and attempt to be the first person to fly an airplane nonstop across the Atlantic Ocean.

By the time he landed at Le Bourget airfield near Paris the next morning, Lindbergh had changed the world of aviation. The attention brought by his flight was unprecedented and dramatically increased public interest in and financial support for air travel. Many have said that no man before or since had done as much for aviation as Lindbergh had with this one flight.

But the flight was just the beginning. Lindbergh had also unwittingly become a world hero and a celebrity. It was not merely his accomplishment that made him a hero. He was also a victorious underdog and a handsome young man who did not drink or smoke. Thus, the press idealized him as an American icon. His timing was also right. According to reporter Fitzhugh Green, Lindbergh provided a hero to the world at a time when the world needed one:

When his plane came to a halt on *Le Bourget* field that black night in Paris, Lindbergh the man kept on going. The phenomenon of Lindbergh took its start with his flight across the ocean; but in its entirety it was almost as distinct from that flight as though he had never flown at all. . . . Perhaps the world was ripe for a youth with a winning smile to flash across its horizon by the brilliance of his achievement momentarily to dim the ugliness of routine business, politics, and crime.[1]

A PRIVATE AND COMPLEX MAN

Following that flight, Lindbergh became a decorated hero. He received the Congressional Medal of Honor, the French Legion of Honor, and the British Air Force Cross. Thousands of writers composed songs and verses in his honor, and he received propositions and job offers that made him a rich man.

But while the press portrayed Lindbergh as a simple icon and hero, historians and biographers have found him much less easy to understand. Historian

Max Lerner says, "Lindbergh was not a simple American boy. I think he was a very complex man . . . and I doubt whether anyone really knew him with the possible exception of his wife. I'm not sure he ever really knew himself."[2]

Indeed, Lindbergh was a private, shy man who did not covet fame or wealth. As a result, the attention of the press and public became a great burden. His daughter Reeve Lindbergh wrote, "Sometimes . . . I wonder whether he would have turned back [on his 1927 flight] if he'd known the life he was heading for."[3] During the next fifteen years of his life, he battled for the privacy and safety of his family and was forced to endure the invasions and harassment of a relentless press.

CONTROVERSIAL FIGURE

Lindbergh also remains a complex and controversial figure for his beliefs and actions. During the late 1930s and early 1940s, he made speeches and wrote articles, primarily anti-Semitic in nature, that offended many people and alienated some of his most fervent supporters and admirers. This course of action, supporting

Legendary American aviator Charles Lindbergh poses beside his small aircraft the Spirit of St. Louis.

views many thought were traitorous, anti-Semitic, and racist, caused Lindbergh to be branded as a villain and Nazi sympathizer by the American press, government, and public.

For this reason, historians, biographers, and others through the years have debated Lindbergh's character. Many have remained critical of his isolationist stance before World War II and his anti-Semitic speeches. Others have forgotten or forgiven him, preferring to remember the young, heroic Lindbergh of 1927. Still others point to the significance of his contributions, isolating Lindbergh the man from his numerous accomplishments.

Clearly, as a public figure, Lindbergh represented many things to different people over time. But the story of Charles Lindbergh the man lies somewhere in between.

1 Fledgling

Charles Augustus Lindbergh was born February 4, 1902, in Detroit, Michigan. He was the only son of Charles August Lindbergh Sr., an attorney and real estate investor from Little Falls, Minnesota, and Evangeline Lodge Land Lindbergh, a schoolteacher from a wealthy family.

Because of his parents' careers and lifestyles, young Charles lived a transient and often lonely childhood. Thus, he was isolated, quiet, and private as a boy and had an unusual degree of self-reliance, patience, and emotional reserve.

ORIGINS

Charles Lindbergh's father, Charles August Lindbergh Sr., called "C.A." all of his adult life, was the son of Ola Månsson, a Swedish immigrant who had been a controversial political figure in his home country. During the 1840s and 1850s, Månsson advocated social reforms and tax relief in Sweden and in doing so made many enemies in the rigid church-controlled government. One of these enemies accused him of embezzling money from the State Bank of Sweden where Månsson worked. Whether or not the charges

were true, Månsson was tried and convicted. Before he could be sentenced, however, he fled Sweden, leaving behind his wife and children because his wife refused to leave the country. Instead, he immigrated to the United States with his mistress Lovisa Callén and their two-year-old son.

Upon arriving in America, Månsson and his new family settled in Stearns County, Minnesota, near the town of Melrose. They immediately applied for American citizenship and changed their Swedish names to more American-sounding ones to better assimilate into their new culture. The couple chose the surname Lindbergh because other immigrants named Månsson before them had done so. Ola Månsson became August Lindbergh, Lovisa Callén became Louisa Carline Lindbergh, and their child, Charles's father, became Charles August (C.A.) Lindbergh.

C.A.

The Lindbergh family lived on the edge of the American wilderness. In his memoirs, Charles Lindbergh wrote that his father's childhood was dangerous and hard. "My father grew up on the frontier. . . . His early boyhood had been spent in constant fear of Indians and reliance upon [U.S.] soldiers."[4] C.A. learned to hunt to provide food for his family, an activity that occupied most of his days. Thus, he had little time for school, attending for the first time when he was in his late teens. C.A. was intelligent, though, and after only two years of high school education entered law school at the University of Michigan in Ann Arbor. After he graduated in 1883, he settled in Little Falls, Minnesota, where he practiced law. There he met Mary LaFond, the daughter of a boardinghouse owner. They married in April 1887.

C.A. and Mary had two daughters, Lillian and Eva, and the family lived well as C.A.'s career prospered. In the 1890s C.A. began investing in real estate around the county and became known as an honest businessman, one with integrity and honor who cared less about money than he did about helping the community thrive. By the late 1890s, C.A. had become one of Little Falls's most well-respected figures.

But the happy times did not last. In 1898 C.A.'s happy family life was destroyed when Mary, several months pregnant, and her unborn child died during an operation to remove a cancerous tumor in her abdomen. Grief-stricken, C.A. took comfort in his daughters and tried to rebuild his life.

EVANGELINE

Two years after his first wife's death, C.A. met and began dating a Little Falls high

Charles Lindbergh Sr. (pictured) attended law school and became a highly regarded businessman.

school chemistry teacher named Evangeline Lodge Land, a twenty-four-year-old woman from Detroit. Evangeline was the daughter of Dr. Charles Henry Land, who invented the porcelain dental crown and many other medical devices and procedures.

Land was an intelligent, energetic, unpredictable woman who had graduated from the University of Michigan with a Bachelor of Science degree in chemistry at a time when many women did not finish high school. After college, she left Detroit to work as a teacher in Little Falls, a town she had never heard of before. Charles Lindbergh recalled that his mother had a romanticized idea about what it would be like to teach in the small rural town. "When she heard of an opening for a chemistry teacher in Little Falls, she visualized a mining town where she would teach the miners' children and walk back and forth to school followed by a big dog carrying her books. She was also attracted by the fact that Little Falls lay across the, to her, highly romantic Mississippi River."[5]

Land's romantic notions did not match the reality of Little Falls, however. She found it difficult to fit in with the community. Her independence and strong personality gave her a reputation around town for being haughty, hot-tempered, and difficult. She also found Little Falls dull after living so many years in the big city of Detroit, and she became very homesick.

In spite of her feelings about the town, she liked C.A. Linbergh. Land was fifteen years younger than Lindbergh but they fell in love and on March 27, 1901, within five months of their first meeting, were married in a small ceremony in her parents' house in Detroit.

C.A. and Evangeline Lindbergh moved back to Minnesota after a ten-week honeymoon spent traveling in the western United States. They settled ten miles from Little Falls, where C.A. bought 120 acres of land. They lived in a rustic cabin for several weeks while workmen built their first house on the banks of the Mississippi River.

Less than a month after their wedding Evangeline became pregnant, and in January 1902 she went to Detroit so that her uncle, a doctor, could deliver the child in the Land family home. The baby came at 1:30 A.M. the morning of February 4. It was a boy who weighed nine and a half pounds. Evangeline named him after her husband, adding the extra syllable "us" to his middle name. He was Charles Augustus Lindbergh.

BOYHOOD ON THE UPPER MISSISSIPPI

When Charles was five weeks old, Evangeline took him back to Minnesota and the completed family home. Living in the large house with the family of five—which included C.A., Evangeline, Lillian, Eva, and baby Charles—were a maid, a cook, and a nurse for the children. The farm's overseer and several workmen lived in a tenant farm across the road.

Charles spent most of his first four years outdoors. His parents thought that fresh air and exercise were important, and Charles was happiest playing outside, learning about wildlife, and daydreaming. He enjoyed collecting butterflies and rocks, and at three years old he tamed a chipmunk; he taught the animal to eat from his hand.

But as idyllic as his childhood seemed, he was lonely. Lillian and Eva were in their teens when Charles was young and were not interested in being his playmates. Thus, he spent most of his time alone or in the company of the family dog. Because of this isolation, according to his sisters, he became painfully shy and remained so throughout his youth.

Charles Lindbergh is pictured with his mother, Evangeline, in 1902.

First Memories

As an adult, Charles had few memories of his early childhood, but one of the first was of his family's home being destroyed by fire when he was three. Charles recalled, "There was sudden shouting—women's voices. I was picked up quickly and taken across the road to a place behind the barn. Somehow I got to the corner of the barn and looked around it to see a huge column of smoke billowing skyward from the corner of the house. Then I was taken back [behind the barn] and told I musn't look."[6] The family escaped unharmed and some of the workmen from the farm helped save some of the family's valuables, but the house was lost.

After the fire, the family moved into a hotel in Uppsala, a town fifteen miles to the south, while the house was rebuilt. However, C.A. had invested most of the family's money in real estate around the county. Therefore, he had little cash and could not afford to construct a new house that was as large as the original. Instead, he built a two-story house on the foundation of the original three-story one.

TURBULENT FAMILY LIFE

Both Charles's parents were reserved people and rarely displayed emotion. They loved their son but were not physically or verbally affectionate with each other or with him. At night, for example, his

Young Lindbergh's parents displayed few emotions other than anger. Eventually, they separated.

mother shook his hand at bedtime rather than kissed him goodnight. His father also encouraged him to control his emotions, to become a rugged and stoic man like himself.

The one emotion Charles's parents did display, however, was anger. Growing up, Charles witnessed his parents' frequent quarrels, which grew worse over time. By the time Charles was four, the marriage had so badly deteriorated that his mother once threatened his father with a gun. C.A. used the loss of the family home as an opportunity to separate from his wife. When it came time for the family to return to the house, he instead took a room in Little Falls near his law office.

CHANGES

In addition to the family's new domestic arrangements, Charles's life changed when his father became interested in politics. In 1906 C.A. successfully campaigned for and won a seat in the U.S. House of Representatives. He represented Minnesota's Sixth Congressional District as a Republican.

Even though Evangeline and C.A.'s marriage was in trouble, Evangeline moved with her young son, Charles, to Washington, D.C., after the election. Lillian and Eva, who did not get along well with their stepmother, moved to Minneapolis, Minnesota, where Lillian was attending college. Evangeline and Charles returned to their Little Falls home during the summers when Congress was not in session, and a nearby farmer who rented land

A YOUNG ENGINEER

Charles Lindbergh proved to be good at science and mechanics early in his life. In his memoir, Boyhood on the Upper Mississippi: A Reminiscent Letter, *he describes how at eight years old he used his skills to come up with a system of slides and pulleys to transport heavy blocks of ice to the house to use as refrigeration.*

"It was my job to fill the [ice]box with ice, and in early years this was a formidable task because of the weight of the ice. (I felt it beneath my dignity to split the cakes in half.)

The icehouse was filled with big ice cakes, cut from the Mississippi [River] in winter from an area above the Little Falls dam. Of course these cakes were always surrounded by sawdust to keep them from melting in the hot summer months. I would shovel the sawdust off a cake, split it carefully into smaller chunks of a size that would just fit into our icebox, and then with a pair of tongs drag one of the chunks up on top of the sawdust. . . .

I had constructed a slide from 2-by-6-inch planks. With a rope attached to the tongs, it was not difficult for me to pull the chunks up the slide. Then I would tip my express cart over on its side, push the ice chunk up against it, and tip the cart upright again. I would pull the cart to a stake in the ground well in front of the kitchen steps, to which I had fastened one end of heavy wire. The other end of the wire I had attached to a ring screw embedded in the house wall above the kitchen porch. I would hook the ice tongs to a pulley that ran over this wire and then haul the pulley with tongs and ice, up on top of the porch. From there it was easy to slide the ice chunk over floors and into the pantry where we kept the ice box. There I had another slide, also made of planks, to get the ice into its compartment."

from the Lindberghs acted as caretaker for the house during the rest of the year.

Evangeline asked C.A. for a divorce soon after she moved to Washington, D.C., but C.A. worried that a divorce would harm his political career. Thus, he refused to give her the divorce. Instead, he asked Evangeline to continue living as they were—married but in separate households—for the sake of his career. In return, he promised to continue providing financially for her and Charles. Evangeline knew that if she fought for divorce in court, she would probably get less money in a divorce settlement than C.A. already provided. Thus, she consented.

A Difficult Childhood

C.A. served in the House of Representatives from 1907 to 1917. During these years Charles and his mother spent summers in Little Falls at the family home and the rest of the year in Washington, D.C., where they lived in a series of boarding-houses. While traveling between the two places, they regularly spent weeks in Detroit visiting Evangeline's family. Charles was happiest at home in Little Falls where he could spend time in nature or at his grandfather's home in Detroit where he could play in his grandfather's home lab-oratory. As Charles recalled, he also dis-liked living in Washington, D.C., because during those months he had to go to school.

Charles entered grammar school in Washington, D.C., in 1909. Although he was intelligent and his mother had taught him basic reading, writing, and arithmetic skills, the transient lifestyle he and Evan-geline led made school difficult for him. His shyness made it hard for him to make friends and he became a loner. He also found it hard to keep up with his classes since he moved so often, regularly arriv-ing for each term late and leaving early.

Charles, pictured with his father, was a shy child and a loner at school.

Additionally, Evangeline enrolled him in different schools each year so he would be near whatever boardinghouse they lived in at the time. For this reason, Charles never stayed in any one school long enough to feel comfortable.

In addition to being a loner at school, Charles was also frequently alone at home. During the long winter months living in boarding houses in Washington, D.C., he was forced to spend much of his time indoors because there was no place for him to play safely outside. Furthermore, since few families or children lived in boardinghouses, he was around adults most of the time, and Evangeline insisted that he play quietly by himself so as not to disturb the other adults.

The boredom of being cooped up inside alone forced Charles to entertain himself with his imagination. During these early years, he began developing a lifelong practice of internal conversations with himself, asking himself a series of

DRIVING

Charles learned to drive his family's first car, a 1912 Model T Ford, when he was eleven years old. As he wrote in his book, Autobiography of Values, *he became the most proficient operator of the car because his parents had trouble learning to drive.*

"[My father] did not like very much to drive. . . . He had had an experience pressing the wrong foot pedal and going backwards instead of forward. Before he got the car under control again, two or three lengths of sheep wire had been torn off the posts of our fence. I was on the back seat when it happened and thought it was awfully funny, but I did not dare to laugh.

My mother also encountered problems driving the car. Speed frightened her so much the first summer that she would never let the clutch pedal out of low gear. . . . The engine got hot and the water in the radiator boiled. It was a sight for the townspeople to see us chugging along so slowly, . . . engine racing and steam snorting from the radiator.

I learned to drive [at eleven]. My eyes could barely see over the steering wheel, but if I sat on a cushion, my feet would not reach break and clutch pedals. . . . [B]y the second summer I had learned to drive with reasonable skill. After that, my parents seldom took the wheel when I was with them. Several years elapsed before my father became accustomed to driving, and my mother remained a rather timid driver."

questions and working out their answers in his head to pass the time. Doing this, he developed a strength of concentration, patience, and an ability to entertain himself for long periods of time without outside stimulus.

ADVENTURES AND TRAVEL

C.A. encouraged his son's solitary existence. His own childhood had been similarly isolated, and he felt that through this experience Charles would become self-reliant and prepared for life's many challenges. "You and I can take hard knocks," he told Charles. "We'll get along no matter what happens."[7]

Even though Charles had to spend much of his younger years alone, he also got to travel more than most children his age. His parents frequently took him on trips to entertain and educate him. One of Charles's first trips with his father was to a 1912 airplane exhibition in Virginia. At such exhibitions, pilots flew the newest planes, did air stunts, and allowed the public to see aircraft up close. Charles was amazed by the demonstration and recalled later that it planted the seed of his love of airplanes. "The experience was so intense and fascinating that I wanted to fly myself,"[8] he recalled.

In 1913 Charles went on another trip, this time to Panama. C.A. was part of a congressional committee overseeing the building of the Panama Canal, an important man-made channel that allows vessels to sail between North and South America. C.A. asked Evangeline to bring

Young Charles's dog Dingo was good company for the lonely boy.

Charles, and the two boarded a ship for Panama where Charles, who loved machines, marveled at the immense construction project. Building the canal involved land movers, cranes, and thousands of engineers and workers.

CARS

After returning from Panama, C.A. bought the family a Model T Ford automobile. Cars at the time were difficult to drive because they required the coordination of pedals and levers in addition to steering.

Charles watched with amusement as his parents struggled to learn to operate the car without much success. When his father first tried backing up he ran into a fence, and when his mother drove she nearly destroyed the engine by driving in low gear until the car overheated. When he was eleven years old Charles got behind the wheel and almost immediately mastered the machine. Soon he did almost all of the driving in the family.

In 1916 C.A. decided to upgrade the family car to a new Ford Saxon Six; the Saxon was easier to drive and had a more

---

MOTHER'S TEMPER

Charles Lindbergh's parents were not emotionally demonstrative people, but his mother, Evangeline Lindbergh, a high school chemistry teacher, had a temper. In his memoir, Boyhood on the Upper Mississippi, *Lindbergh describes one example of his mother's losing her temper that ended her teaching career in Little Falls, Minnesota.*

"[My mother's] chemistry laboratory was on the top floor of the high school in a sort of 'attic room.' It was not well heated. One sub-zero winter day, my mother concluded that the room was too cold for her students and proceeded to carry the apparatus she wanted to demonstrate to her chemistry class downstairs. This was against school regulations. On the stairs she met the high school superintendent, who said she would have to take the apparatus back to the attic. She said the attic was too cold and proceeded to continue downstairs.

The superintendent blocked her way. My mother's flashing Irish temper rose. She put the apparatus on the stairs in front of the superintendent, walked out of the school, and never taught there again."

Evangeline Lindbergh in 1920.

powerful motor. Charles, then fourteen years old, learned not only to drive the new car but to take it apart and service it. He became so proficient at both activities that in the summer of 1916 he drove his mother and uncle to California to visit Lillian, who had moved there after college.

The trip from Little Falls to Los Angeles was long and arduous. In 1916 there were no highways and most roads were unpaved. During wet or cold weather, the roads frequently washed out or became so muddy that they were difficult to drive over. Charles recalled the trip as treacherous and slow because of the road conditions: "There were rainy days in Missouri when mud collected on the Saxon's wheels until we could not move. Frozen ruts in New Mexico slowed us down to a speed of less than ten miles an hour, as did the Arizona sand. Frequent trouble . . . delayed us for hours that added up to days."[9] The trip took forty days, but Charles was a capable driver and mechanic who got the car and its passengers safely to Los Angeles.

Evangeline liked the West Coast, and soon after their arrival decided to stay for a few months, perhaps indefinitely. Thus, Charles again entered a new school. He started eleventh grade at Redondo Union High School in Redondo Beach, a suburb of Los Angeles. As always, Charles spent his time at school alone and did not do well with his studies. But he enjoyed spending time with his mother and uncle and liked taking trips to San Diego, San Francisco, and Catalina Island.

Evangeline and Charles remained in California until April 1917. That year,

Evangeline's mother fell ill with cancer and needed her daughter to care for her. Charles's uncle took a train back to Minnesota to attend to Charles's grandmother while Charles drove his mother back to Little Falls.

FARMING

In 1917 the United States entered World War I. An isolationist who had struggled to keep America out of the conflict, C.A. quit politics and began traveling around the country looking for business ventures. Although this meant he had to be away from Charles and Evangeline, he did not mind because he felt his son had grown up and no longer needed his guidance. He saw Charles, only fifteen years old, as a capable, hard working man with whom he could entrust the management of the family farm and land. Thus, C.A. deeded over much of the 120-acre farm to Charles.

Although Charles was undoubtably pleased with his father's faith in him, this presented problems. Already struggling through his senior year in high school, Charles began running the farm in addition to helping to take care of his mother and ailing grandmother, who had come to live with them. Furthermore, for the first time in his life, Charles had begun to excel in two subjects that appealed to him, physics and mechanical drawing, for which he seemed to have a natural talent. But the responsibilities of the farm made it difficult for him to maintain his new interest in school. He recalled:

GOD, AS REMOTE AS THE STARS

Neither of Charles Lindbergh's parents were religious, so Charles was raised without much formal religious guidance or instruction. In 1907, however, when his father was elected to Congress, the family attended church together for the first time in an effort to please C.A. Lindbergh's religious supporters. Charles disliked church, however. He found it boring and thought it was a waste of time. But he spent much of his life thinking about God and religion. In his book The Spirit of St. Louis, *he remembers some of his early experiences with religion.*

"Through the years of my childhood, church was an ordeal to be cautiously avoided. God remained vague and disturbing. You heard of Him in story books, in the cursing of lumberjacks, in the blessing of an old aunt. No one could tell you what He looked like, and He seemed to have a lot to do with people who died. . . . I pictured Him as a stern old man living in Heaven, somewhere off in the sky like clouds; knowing about and judging your every act. . . .

On the sleeping porch of our . . . house, I lay awake in the evenings, staring out at the sky, thinking about God and life and death. One might meet God after one died, I decided, but He didn't have much to do with life; no one I knew had ever seen Him, and the people who didn't believe in Him seemed to get along as well as those who did. . . .But if there were a God, how did He begin? . . . If God existed, why didn't He show Himself to people, so there'd be no argument about it? No, God was as remote as the stars, and less real—you could see the stars on a clear night; but you never saw God."

I found school difficult that winter, especially so because of my attraction to the farm. I got along fairly well in physics and mechanical drawing. Other subjects I found more tedious, and for me much homework seemed impossible. When I returned to the farm after school, there were always outdoor duties pressing, more essential and attractive than schoolwork. When they were finished and supper eaten, I was usually too sleepy to read many pages in my textbooks.[10]

As a result of his many responsibilities, Charles's grades suffered, and it looked as though he was not going to be able to graduate. However, the United States involvement in World War I required a great increase in the production of food, and in support of this effort, the principal of Charles's high school announced that any boy wishing to do volunteer farm work for the cause would receive full school credit. For Charles, a senior, it meant that he could be excused from taking final examinations and be awarded a high school diploma. Charles took the opportunity and left school to work on the farm full time.

In the year that he ran the farm, Charles increased the farm's productivity. He bred cattle, hogs, sheep, chickens, and geese, spending most of his days working long, exhausting hours caring for the animals. Then, in June 1918 he graduated on time with his high school class; graduating at sixteen was common in the early twentieth century. He made one last trip to school to pick up his diploma.

CHANGING PLANS

After graduation, Charles continued his work on the farm and made plans to enlist in the armed services in 1920 after his eighteenth birthday. He spent his evenings reading a serial comic strip called *Tam o' the Scoots* about a heroic World War I pilot. The story enthralled him. Charles wanted to become a pilot, and he thought the war would give him the opportunity to learn to fly. "[Tam o' the Scoots] represented chivalry and daring in my own day as did King Arthur's knights in childhood stories. If I joined the Army," he later wrote, "I would apply for the branch of aviation and, if possible, learn to be the pilot of a scout [a pilot who flew ahead of the ground troops to gather information about the enemy's position and defenses]."[11]

Charles never did get the opportunity to fight in World War I. On November 11, 1918, the war ended. Additionally, the farm was no longer needed for the war effort, so Charles sold the livestock and machinery. He kept the house and rented out the farmland. He used some of the money he made to buy himself a motor-cycle, a twin-cylinder Excelsior, and took several trips around the country.

In the first years after the war, Charles's life was in transition. He still wanted to become a pilot, but he was unsure of how to go about it. His parents, on the other hand, encouraged him to think about college, even though he had never been a good student. Although he did not look forward to school, Charles did not know what else to do. So he took his parents' advice and enrolled at the University of Wisconsin at Madison; he decided to study mechanical engineering.

In fall 1920 Charles left Little Falls and traveled to Madison. Evangeline's mother had passed away the year before, and without Charles at the farm Evangeline felt she had no reason to stay. She decided to follow Charles to Madison.

COLLEGE

Evangeline and Charles moved into an apartment near the university. Charles liked the campus. The natural setting with its wooded lakeshore trails and outdoor activities appealed to him.

When classes began, Charles enrolled in chemistry, drawing, English, and mathematics. He disliked the classes though, preferring to spend time outdoors around the many woods and lakes near the school. And he neglected his studies. Charles was frustrated with the required introductory courses. Instead, he wanted to get to the engineering classes that he was most interested in. He said,

> Why should one spend the hours of life on [grammar], semi-colons, and our crazy English spelling? . . . God [did not make] man to fiddle with pencil marks on paper. He gave him earth and air to feel. And now wings with which to fly. I'd like to stop taking English and concentrate on engineering. Then, maybe I could take an aeronautical engineering course. I believe I'd be more successful in that.[12]

Lindbergh sits atop his Excelsior motorcycle in 1921.

FLUNKING OUT

There was one college activity at which Charles excelled: the Reserve Officer Training Corps (ROTC) program, in which college students trained as soldiers in preparation for careers in the military. Charles enjoyed the discipline and the routine of soldiering. Through the ROTC, he joined the University of Wisconsin's rifle and pistol squad and regularly shot perfect scores during drills.

Charles's academic work did not improve, however. He was placed on academic probation for failing in English and doing poorly in chemistry and math, which meant that he would be expelled if his grades did not improve within the next term. Adding to his problems in school was the fact that his father was doing poorly in his business ventures and was deeply in debt. C.A. told his son that he might not be able to afford Charles's tuition payments at the University of Wisconsin for much longer.

By summer 1921 Charles was so frustrated he considered dropping out of college. But he did not want to quit, feeling that it would disappoint his parents. He returned for his second year to give school another try. He tried to get interested in the courses and to work harder, but he soon returned to his old habits of cutting class.

Finally, in the winter of 1921, Charles decided that college was not for him. He

Lindbergh (third from right) poses with members of the University of Wisconsin's ROTC rifle and pistol squad. The young man excelled at marksmanship.

wanted to become a pilot and decided to find a way to achieve that goal. He wrote letters to flying schools all over the country and was accepted at the flight school run by a small aircraft manufacturing company, the Nebraska Aircraft Corporation in Lincoln, Nebraska. For five hundred dollars, the school would teach him all aspects of building, repairing, and flying planes over a period of three months. Then when he received his semester grades, Charles quit school. He had failed three of his courses.

Following a Dream

When he told his mother of his plans to quit school, she supported him. Although she valued education, she understood that flying was important to her son and encouraged him to do what he thought best. "You must go," she said. "You must lead your own life. I musn't hold you back."[13] His father was less enthusiastic but no less supportive. Remembered Charles, "He [C.A.] spoke of the danger of aviation, and told me there would always be a place for me in his business if I wanted it; but he did not argue against my decision."[14]

In fact, C.A. agreed to pay for flight school with the understanding that Charles would attend the University of Nebraska in Lincoln once he completed the flying courses. Charles agreed to the terms and dropped out of the University of Wisconsin. In March 1922 he rode his motorcycle south toward Lincoln, Nebraska, to become a pilot.

2 Taking Flight

In the early to mid-1920s Charles Lindbergh held various jobs associated with piloting. His transient youth had made him a restless young man, and he rarely held a job for very long. He cared little about money, and once he mastered a task or a skill, he became bored and sought new adventures and challenges. This restlessness led Lindbergh to consider what would be the key challenge of his life: piloting the first nonstop transatlantic flight in 1927.

"A God's Eye View"

Lindbergh arrived in Lincoln, Nebraska, in April 1922 and reported to Nebraska Aircraft for the first day of classes. Upon arrival, he was surprised to find the company had been sold and the new owner, an entrepreneur named Ray Page, had forgotten to make arrangements for flight school classes. Lindbergh had been the first and only student to sign up for the term and was the only one to show up for instruction.

Nonetheless, Lindbergh was eager to start learning about airplanes, and Page put him to work. The company refur-bished and modernized old planes in order to sell them, and Lindbergh got the opportunity to work at every job that was required to rebuild aircraft, from disassembling motors to applying varnish to the fabric of airplane wings to make them strong and waterproof.

Instruction at Nebraska Aircraft was informal and haphazard. There were no classes or lectures. Instead, Lindbergh had to pick up knowledge by asking questions of the company's mechanics and by hands-on experimentation. Although Lindbergh thought many people would find some of the work dull, he was fascinated. "So far I have had work that is not very exciting," Lindbergh wrote in a letter to his mother, "but interesting to *me*."[15]

In his second week at the factory, he helped prepare one of the company's refurbished twin cockpit biplanes for its first flight. On April 9 the plane was ready, and Otto Timm, the company's chief engineer and pilot, offered to take Lindbergh up for his first flight. Lindbergh and another factory worker sat together in the front cockpit while Timm piloted from the rear. The fifteen-minute flight was beyond Lindbergh's expectations and made certain his desire to become a pilot. He recalled: "[It] seemed an experience beyond mortality. There was the earth spreading out below me, a planet where I had lived but from which I had astonishingly risen. It had been the home of my body. I felt strangely apart from my body in the plane. I was never more aware of all existence, never less aware of myself. Mine was a god's eye view."[16]

BARNSTORMING AND WINGWALKING

Lindbergh was thrilled by his flying experience and in late April began taking piloting lessons. His flight instructor was Ira O. "Biff" Biffle who taught army pilots during World War I. Lindbergh logged almost eight hours of instruction by late May when Biffle announced that Lind-

bergh was proficient enough to pilot the plane alone.

But Lindbergh did not get the chance to fly solo at that time. He was an inexperienced pilot, and Page was worried Lindbergh might wreck the plane. Thus, Page told Lindbergh he would have to pay a cash bond to insure against any possible damage to the plane, but Lindbergh could not afford it. Another obstacle arose when Page negotiated the sale of the plane—the only instruction craft the company owned. That meant Lindbergh would get no further flying instruction in the air.

The buyer of the plane, a pilot named Erold G. Bahl, planned to use it to go barnstorming through southern Nebraska. "Barnstorming" is an aviator's term that means flying from town to town to give air shows and sightseeing flights for money. Many pilots in the 1920s made money barnstorming, and it seemed a romantic

Lindbergh in 1923. Fascinated with flying, Lindbergh began taking flying lessons.

THE LIFE OF AN AVIATOR

Lindbergh never regretted his decision to drop out of the University of Wisconsin to pursue his dream of becoming a pilot. In his memoir, Autobiography of Values, *he writes that aviation was an unusual and dangerous profession in the 1920s, but that to him the challenge, excitement, and beauty of the life far outweighed the risks.*

"The life of an aviator seemed to me ideal. It involved skill. It commanded adventure. It made use of the latest developments in science. I was glad I had failed my college courses. Mechanical engineers were fettered [tied] to factories and drafting boards, while pilots had the freedom of the wind in the expanse of sky. . . . There were times in an airplane when it seemed I had partially escaped mortality, to look down on the earth like a god. . . .

It was true that aviation was dangerous. Talks of pilots and airplanes almost always included accounts of fatal crashes. . . . It was commonly said that anyone entering aviation did not place much value on his life.

But how was one to measure the preciousness of life? . . . Was it not better to enjoy living even though life might be cut short as a result? I believed the value of life related to its quality as well as to its duration. . . . Of course I would like to become a centenarian [live to be one hundred years old], but I decided that ten years spent as the pilot of an airplane was in value worth more than an ordinary lifetime."

and adventurous life to Lindbergh. Certain he would never get a pilot's job with only eight hours in-flight instruction to his record, Lindbergh asked Bahl if he could go with him as an unpaid assistant and mechanic. That way, he could get some more time in the air. Bahl agreed, and the two left Lincoln in early May.

Lindbergh enjoyed barnstorming. He loved flying more than anything he had ever experienced and savored every moment in the air. Additionally, he liked the work he did on the ground, tinkering with the plane and talking with the farmers and townspeople he and Bahl performed for.

Soon after he began flying with Bahl, Lindbergh had an idea of attracting more customers by doing a popular air stunt called wing walking. During the stunt, he climbed onto the biplane's top wing and rode on it as he and Bahl flew into towns. The stunt was dangerous; it required good balance and the willingness to risk what would almost surely be a fatal fall. But for these same reasons the stunt was very popular among crowds. So Lindbergh did it.

DAREDEVIL LINDBERGH

Lindbergh returned to Lincoln in June 1922, determined to buy his own plane. He had almost no money, though, so he picked up work at Page's aircraft factory again, doing odd jobs for fifteen dollars a week. While working there, he saw a parachute exhibition given by a parachute salesman, Charles Hardin. Lindbergh was fascinated by the exhibition and asked Hardin to teach him to jump. Hardin liked Lindbergh and saw a potential customer, so he agreed. The next afternoon Lindbergh successfully performed his first jump.

Parachutes were not common at the time and were considered dangerous. Thus, Lindbergh earned some local notoriety as a daredevil for the jump. Two weeks later, Lindbergh went barnstorming with a pilot who had been impressed by his bravery and offered him a job. Lindbergh toured with the pilot for four months in Colorado, Kansas, Nebraska, Wyoming, and ended up in Montana. Billed on advertisement flyers as "Daredevil Lindbergh," he worked as a mechanic, wing walker, and stunt parachutist.

NEW CHALLENGES

As enjoyable as barnstorming was, Lindbergh soon became restless and wanted a new challenge. Foremost, he wanted to finish his pilot training and buy his own plane. Over the four months he spent barnstorming in the West and Midwest, he saved as much of his money as he could for the purchase.

When the barnstorming season ended in October 1922, Lindbergh still did not have enough to buy a plane. He also had no immediate plans for the future. His parents encouraged him to return to school. But although he had promised his father he would go back to college, Lindbergh enjoyed the life he was living and had no intention of returning to school. Instead, he spent the winter of 1922 visiting his parents in Detroit and Minneapolis. His mother had moved back to Michigan to be close to her family home, and C.A. was living in a cheap hotel in Minneapolis, having been driven deeply into debt by bad business investments.

Charles Lindbergh spent many hours talking with his parents about his adventures, about airplanes, and about his desire to buy one. C.A. realized that his son was serious about being a pilot. Thus, even though he was in financial trouble, C.A. cosigned a loan with his son toward the purchase of a plane.

JENNY

On April 20, 1923, Charles Lindbergh headed south to find himself a plane. He took a train to Americus, Georgia, where the government auctioned off World War I planes nicknamed "Jennies" and businesses refurbished and sold them to the public. Lindbergh purchased a reconstructed Jenny for one thousand dollars and then waited in Americus while mechanics fitted the plane to his specifications. Two weeks later the plane was ready. When the mechanics brought it out to the

Lindbergh's World War I Jenny in 1923. The plane is pictured after a minor crash near Glencoe, Minnesota.

runway for him, Lindbergh was excited but realized that he had a problem. He recalled, "I had never been up in a plane alone. . . . No one on the field knew that I had never soloed. . . . I did not have sufficient money to pay for more instruction, so one day I taxied to one end of the field, opened the throttle, and started to take off."[17]

Because of high winds his first attempt to take off was unsuccessful. An experienced pilot saw his trouble and told him to wait until evening when the winds died down. Lindbergh took the advice and tried again that evening. Then, he successfully took off on his first attempt. He later wrote that the flight was unforgettable:

> The first solo flight is one of the events in a pilot's life which forever remains impressed on his memory. It is the culmination of difficult hours of instruction, hard weeks of training and often years of anticipation. To be absolutely alone for the first time in the cockpit of a plane hundreds of feet above the ground is an experience never to be forgotten.[18]

MAKING A LIVING

After a week of practicing takeoffs and landings in Americus, Georgia, Lindbergh headed home, barnstorming his way north. He found barnstorming on his own difficult, though, because there were so many pilots competing for work. Often he would arrive in town to find that a barnstormer had just left, taking with him the town's enthusiasm and money.

Thus, Lindbergh spent the late spring and early summer of 1923 in various towns, doing odd jobs when he could not make money barnstorming. He worked as a handyman, a flying instructor, and a gas station attendant. He also received a request that summer from his father, who had decided to give politics one more try.

C.A. asked his son to fly him around Minnesota to campaign for the Senate. Charles Lindbergh agreed and gave his father his first ride in an airplane. The two men spent several weeks together, flying over the state, dropping leaflets, campaigning, and enjoying each other's company.

A few weeks later Lindbergh also flew with his mother, taking her barnstorming with him through Iowa and Wisconsin for ten days. Evangeline enjoyed flying from the start, and she helped her son advertise his barnstorming flights. Flying with her son also alleviated her concerns about his not attending college. She had never seen him as happy.

ARMY CADET

Happy as he was, though, Lindbergh again became restless. Once he felt he had

---

ROUGH RIDE DOWN THE YELLOWSTONE

After barnstorming through several states with another pilot in 1923, Lindbergh ended up in Montana. Deciding to make an adventure of his return to Nebraska, he bought a small boat for two dollars and planned to sail down the Yellowstone River to Lincoln, Nebraska. But, as Lindbergh describes in his book We, *the journey did not last long.*

"I started alone down the Yellowstone River on the way to Lincoln. The river was not deep and ran over numerous rapids which were so shallow that even the flat bottom of my boat would bump over the rocks from time to time. I had been unable to purchase a thoroughly seagoing vessel . . . and very little rough going was required to knock out the resin from [old sealed] cracks and open the old leaks again. . . .

As I progressed downstream through the ever-present rapids, more and more of my time was required for bailing out the boat with an old tin can, until at the end of the first day, when I had traveled about twenty miles, I was spending fully half of my time bailing out water. . . .

The next morning . . . rain set in, and this together with the water from the ever-increasing leaks in the sides and bottom of the boat required such constant bailing that I found little use for the oars that day. By evening the rocks had taken so much effect that the boat was practically beyond repair. . . . I traded what was left of the boat to a son of a nearby rancher for a wagon ride to the nearest town, Huntley, Montana. I expressed [shipped] my [camping] equipment and bought a railroad ticket to Lincoln."

mastered barnstorming and stunt flying, he went looking for a new challenge. He wanted to become a world-class pilot and realized that flying only his Jenny, which was a simple and outdated plane, limited his skills. Further, barnstorming was primarily a job for money, and the pursuit of money was not his primary interest. "[New flying] opportunities were more desirable than money,"[19] he wrote.

In October 1923, in search of new opportunities and challenges, Lindbergh flew to Lambert Field, a busy airfield in St. Louis, Missouri, to attend the International Air Races. The event was an exhibition at which the public could view the newest

Lindbergh was assigned the rank of second lieutenant in the Air Service Reserve Corps after graduating Army flight school.

models and designs of planes in flight, examine them on the ground, and talk with their pilots. Lindbergh was awestruck by the range and abilities of the new planes. He very much wanted to get the chance to fly them, but they were far too expensive for him to purchase, and many of them were so technically complex that they required more advanced piloting skills than he had, even if he could have afforded them. One of the pilots at the field suggested that Lindbergh join the army. "Why don't you sign up with the Army as an air cadet?" he suggested. "You get all the flying you want—and they pay for it."[20]

Lindbergh took the advice and enrolled as a U.S. Army Air Service Reserve cadet. He wrote away for an application in January 1924 and reported to Brooks Field in San Antonio, Texas, on March 15 for exams and a physical. He passed the exams and physical and was inducted, or accepted, into the army. He was one of more than a hundred new cadets.

Although Lindbergh was enthusiastic about his acceptance, the reality of the training was a shock; he soon learned how much academic work was expected of him during his one-year training. Each afternoon was spent in the classroom, and he was required to study twenty-five difficult subjects. If he failed only three of these, he would be asked to leave the program. Lindbergh had never done well in school. He was never able to concentrate or keep his mind from wandering, but he realized quickly that to succeed he had to focus and work hard.

Lindbergh focused on his studies to the exclusion of all other activities and found

PRACTICAL JOKER

Although he had been a quiet loner for most of his youth and young adulthood, Charles Lindbergh always had a good sense of humor. While training as a pilot in the U.S. Army Flight School, Lindbergh became the practical joker of his barracks. In his book Lindbergh, *biographer A. Scott Berg describes some of Lindbergh's exploits.*

"[Lindbergh became] the practical joker of 'the gang'—dumping a fellow cadet's gear in the middle of the barracks, removing another's to a rooftop, turning a hose on in the bed of a sound sleeper, putting shaving cream into the open mouth of a snorer, dousing a sergeant's pillow with skunk 'juice' [the foul smelling liquid that skunks excrete]. . . . He bragged to his mother . . . that he fed an arrogant loudmouth at the field some laxative tablets, passing them off as candy; and he exploded a stink bomb in a man's flight suit glove. Lindbergh also delighted for decades in the time he got [a friend] to swallow two big gulps of kerosene, having led him to believe it was water."

school rewarding. He studied long hours, even on weekends and in the evenings. All of his studying paid off. He did well and for the first time felt rewarded for classroom work. What he learned meant something to him. He wrote, "The Army schools taught me what I had never learned before—how to study, even subjects in which I had no interest. For the first time in my experience, school and life became both rationally and emotionally connected."[21]

FATHER'S DEATH

Less than a month into his training, Lindbergh received a telegram from his half-sister Eva in Minnesota. It said that his father was critically ill, suffering from a brain tumor, and was in intensive care at the Mayo Clinic hospital in Rochester, Minnesota.

Although he risked failing at school if he missed a portion of his training, Lindbergh requested emergency leave and rushed to Minnesota by train. When he arrived in Rochester, doctors told him that his father was not expected to live more than a few weeks. Lindbergh had not expected such a grave diagnosis. He wrote,

Their report was a terrific shock to me, for the last letter my father wrote contained no warning of illness. Apparently he did not realize it himself until a friend noticed a blank area in the usual acuteness of his mind and insisted that he undergo medical examination. Now, he could not even speak. But he recognized me at his bedside and took my hand.[22]

Lindbergh had been given only ten days leave and, feeling there was nothing he could do for his father, he returned to Texas. The next month, on May 24, 1924, C.A. Lindbergh died. He was sixty-five years old.

LIEUTENANT "BEANS" LINDBERGH

Like his mother and father, Lindbergh was not comfortable showing his emotions, and he spoke little about his father's death. Rather, he distracted himself by focusing on his studies and quickly caught up with the work he had missed.

Lindbergh's commitment to his studies was reflected in his high grades, and when the nineteen remaining cadets graduated in May 1925, Lindbergh was at the top of the class. After graduation, like all successful officer candidates, he was given the rank of second lieutenant in the Air Service Reserve Corps.

The army, however, did not need new pilots at the time, so instead of receiving a military assignment, he had to find civilian work. The city that attracted him most was St. Louis, where he had attended the International Air Races in 1923. Many job opportunities existed there, and the city had become a popular aviation intersection for the nation's air traffic.

Lindbergh took a train from Dallas to St. Louis and moved into a boardinghouse near Lambert Field. Almost immediately, he was offered a job. Frank and William Robertson, two World War I pilots who had started their own aircraft company, Robertson Aircraft, offered Lindbergh a position as chief pilot for a new airmail route from St. Louis to Chicago. He would be one of the first pilots in the nation to fly mail from one city to the next for a civilian company. Up to that time, only army pilots had delivered airmail, and the government was turning the service over to nonmilitary companies for the first time.

Robertson Aircraft had not yet received its permission from the government to fly the route, however. Thus, even though Lindbergh wanted the job, there would be a delay of weeks, perhaps months, before he could start. Needing to work, Lindbergh barnstormed for several weeks and joined a flying circus as a stunt pilot and wing walker; he was billed as "Beans" Lindbergh. In June, after the circus finished its month-long tour, Lindbergh returned to St. Louis, knowing it was the best place in the country to find work as a pilot. For the next year he worked in the air wherever he could.

AIRMAIL PILOT

In April 1926, the government contract for Robertson Aircraft came through and the company was ready for operation. On April 15, at 5:50 A.M., Lindbergh took off on his first airmail delivery from St. Louis to Illinois. The airmail planes were converted twin cockpit planes; the front cockpit had been converted into a compartment to hold the bags of mail. Lindbergh and his crew of three other pilots were responsible for five round-trip deliveries. Working on rotating shifts, the pilots flew from one airfield to the next, where they were met by a postal truck with a load of airmail letters.

The job was challenging and dangerous because the planes were old and prone to crashing; they had been nicknamed "flying coffins" by the pilots. Additionally, pilots had to navigate the planes by sight since the company could not afford to buy proper navigating equipment. While flying by sight was not a problem during the summer when the days were long, during the winters Lindbergh and the other pilots frequently had to fly in darkness, using emergency flares and a pocket flashlight to guide them. They landed in narrow cow pastures or fields lit by floodlights.

In spite of the danger of the job, after a year Lindbergh felt he had mastered the challenges of flying the airmail route and became bored with the routine. Flying back and forth over the same routes offered him little challenge, and he thought flying had become too easy. Lindbergh wrote, "There's no ability required in holding your course over familiar country with a sharp horizon in every quarter. . . . To be a pilot of the night mail appeared [at one time] the summit of ambition for a flyer; yet here I am, in the cockpit of a mail plane boring through the night."[23]

Lindbergh (seated, right) served as one of the first U.S. airmail pilots, flying decrepit planes nicknamed "flying coffins."

JUMPING TO SAFETY

During his aviation training and career as a test pilot and airmail carrier, Charles Lindbergh escaped by parachute from four dangerous crashes. In November 1926, after his fourth emergency jump, he was recognized for setting the world record for emergency jumps.

In his book The Spirit of St. Louis, *Lindbergh describes his third emergency jump, which occurred on September 16, 1926. While flying through nighttime fog, his airmail plane ran out of fuel; its 110 gallon fuel tank had been replaced with a much smaller tank during repairs but Lindbergh had not been notified of the change.*

"At 5,000 feet the engine sputtered and died. I stepped . . . out over the right side of the cockpit, pulling the [parachute] ripcord after about a 100-foot fall. The parachute . . . functioned perfectly; I was falling head downward when the risers jerked me into an upright position and the chute opened. . . . I pulled [my] flashlight from my belt and was playing it down towards the top of the fog when I heard the plane's engine pick up. When I jumped it had practically stopped dead and I had neglected to cut the switches. Apparently when the ship nosed down an additional supply of gasoline drained to the carburetor. Soon [the plane] came into sight, about a quarter mile away and headed in the general direction of my parachute. . . . The plane . . . passed approximately 300 yards away from my chute."

Lindbergh (fourth from left) stands at the site of his 1926 airmail plane wreck. Lindbergh escaped from the plane by parachute.

While on his many monotonous trips between St. Louis and his Illinois stops, Lindbergh daydreamed, considering the ways of extending a pilot's time in the air. At the time, planes could fly only several hundred miles at a time; even the best planes of the day could not support the weight of the gasoline required for longer distances. The challenge of figuring out how to extend the distance of a flight thrilled Lindbergh. "Suppose I really could stay up here and keep on flying; suppose gasoline didn't weigh so much and I could put enough in the tanks to last for days. . . . I could fly anywhere I wanted—anywhere in the world—to the North Pole or to China or to some jungle island if I wished."[24]

EYE ON THE ORTEIG PRIZE

Lindbergh's ideas about extending the length of flight led him to consider trying for the Orteig Prize, named for a French-born American hotel owner named Raymond Orteig. In 1919, in celebration of the French and American victory over Germany in World War I, Orteig had offered twenty-five thousand dollars to any aviator who could fly across the Atlantic Ocean from New York to Paris or Paris to New York in one flight, symbolically joining France and America.

Lindbergh learned about the Orteig Prize when he saw a September 1926 newsreel about French captain René Fonck's recent unsuccessful attempt to make the transatlantic flight. Fonck's plane, a large three-engine craft weighing twenty-eight thousand pounds, crashed during takeoff, killing two of the four crew members. After seeing the newsreel, Lindbergh came up with the idea of using a single-engine plane in which a pilot flew solo rather than with a crew. This, Lindbergh theorized, would reduce the load of the plane and reduce the amount of fuel required by additional engines. These factors, he believed, would sufficiently prolong the plane's fuel reserves so it could cross the Atlantic.

Flying alone, however, would mean staying awake for thirty to forty hours, the amount of time the flight would take. Lindbergh weighed that challenge against his own abilities and experience and decided to go for the prize. He wrote,

> Why shouldn't I fly from New York to Paris? I'm almost twenty-five. I have more than four years of aviation behind me, and close to two thousand hours in the air. I've barnstormed over half of the forty-eight states. I've flown my mail through the worst of nights. I know the wind currents of the Rocky Mountains and the storms of the Mississippi Valley as few pilots know them. . . . Why am I not qualified for such a flight? . . . Why wouldn't a flight across the ocean prove as possible as [past challenges] have been? As I attempted them, I can—I will attempt that too. I'll organize a flight to Paris![25]

3 Preparations

Lindbergh's decision to attempt to win the Orteig Prize brought about his most difficult challenge to that time. He knew the transatlantic flight would be a difficult endeavor, but he did not anticipate the many disappointments, aggravations, and setbacks he encountered as he prepared to cross the ocean. Even so, during the months spent preparing for his journey Lindbergh overcame doubts, fears, and problems with resolve, persistence, and determination.

RAISING FUNDS

In 1926, when Lindbergh chose to try for the Orteig Prize, he realized that making the decision was only the first step of many toward accomplishing his goal. The first obstacle to overcome was money. Although he had almost two thousand dollars in savings, he knew a new plane would cost at least ten thousand dollars. That meant he had to raise the money from people interested in investing in his flight.

In his search for investors, Lindbergh made appointments with some of the wealthiest buisnessmen in St. Louis. His first was with Major Albert B. Lambert in St. Louis. Lambert was an aviation pioneer

after whom Lambert Field was named. Lambert admired Lindbergh's enthusiasm and pledged one thousand dollars. Lambert also said that his brother, another aviation enthusiast, would match the amount.

Despite this early success, Lindbergh found many others less eager to support his venture. Several possible investors were astonished that he thought he could cross the Atlantic by himself in a small plane when larger planes with more experienced pilots had failed. Many said that they could not fund such a mission. The owners of the St. Louis newspaper, *Post-Dispatch*, for example, said they could not possibly endorse the flight; they were sure that Lindbergh would crash and bring them bad publicity.

Lindbergh persevered, however, and after weeks of setbacks his work paid off. Several individuals, including his bosses at Robertson Aircraft, finally agreed to back him. With their help Lindbergh amassed fifteen thousand dollars to fund the flight.

FRUSTRATION

Raising the money was just the first step. Lindbergh knew that finding a suitable and available aircraft would prove even more difficult. Any company that sold him a plane gambled its reputation on the success of his flight. As with his investors, Lindbergh had to convince aviation executives of his abilities before they would agree to help him.

One aviation company after another turned him down. Although he was an accomplished pilot at age twenty-four, Lindbergh was not famous and still looked too young for most of the executives to believe that he was qualified. Furthermore, many of them thought his plans were absurd. Thus, by winter 1926 Lindbergh was discouraged by his failure to find a plane. So, he decided to have a plane built from

Lindbergh in 1930. Three years earlier Lindbergh designed his custom monoplane.

scratch. By building a plane of his own design, he would not have to worry about companies wanting to stake their reputations on his success or failure.

RACING AHEAD

Lindbergh was not the only pilot who wanted to win the Orteig Prize. Among his competitors were some world-famous figures, including U.S. Navy commander Richard Evelyn Byrd, who had become the first man to fly over the North Pole in 1926, and René Fonck, who had made an unsuccessful attempt at the Orteig Prize in September 1926. Additionally, a French pilot named Charles Nungesser and his copilot, François Coli, were preparing their plane, *White Bird*, for an attempt in spring of 1927.

In January 1927, with the urgency of beating his competition driving him, Lindbergh contacted aircraft manufacturers all over the country in search of one who would agree to build the plane he needed for the price he could afford. Only one company responded positively. A small manufacturer, the Ryan Aircraft Company, in San Diego, California, said that for just over ten thousand dollars they could build a redesigned monoplane with a range of four thousand miles and fitted with the motor and navigation instruments Lindbergh wanted. Unfortunately, it would take three months to build. Lindbergh worried that one of his competitors would have completed the flight by then.

Discouraged, Lindbergh met with one of his investors, Harry Knight, to discuss

Lindbergh was frustrated by his early failures to raise investment funds to buy a plane for his 1927 transatlantic flight. In his journal, published in the book The Spirit of St. Louis, *Lindbergh complains about the setbacks he was suffering.*

"I've found no one willing to take part in financing a flight across the ocean. The men I've talked to who are interested don't have enough money. Those who have enough consider the risk too great—if not for their bank accounts then for their reputations. I've not been able to convince them that flying the ocean is no more dangerous than [flying during] winter on the mail [routes]. They want no share in the criticism they think would come from sending a young pilot to his death."

the problem. During the meeting, Lindbergh suggested that they forget about the Orteig Prize and focus their efforts on another project; possibly he could make a transpacific flight later in the year. Knight, however, seeing how disappointed Lindbergh seemed, refused to let him give up. Knight said, "He [Lindbergh] had set his heart on winning the Orteig Prize, and now here he was telling me he was ready to give it up. I wasn't going to let him. I said: 'Let's stick to the Paris flight, Slim. That's the idea we started out with.'"[26]

SUCCESS

Lindbergh's morale improved after his meeting with Knight. He spent the month of February in San Diego negotiating with Ryan Aircraft. Near the end of the month, Ryan Aircraft altered its original estimate and agreed to build the plane in two months by working crews around the

clock. Lindbergh sent a telegram to his St. Louis investors telling them the good news. It read,

BELIEVE RYAN CAPABLE OF BUILDING PLANE WITH SUFFICIENT PERFORMANCE STOP COST COMPLETE WITH WHIRLWIND ENGINE AND STANDARD INSTRUMENTS IS TEN THOUSAND FIVE HUNDRED EIGHTY DOLLARS STOP DELIVERY WITHIN SIXTY DAYS STOP RECOMMEND CLOSING DEAL—LINDBERGH.[27]

His investors wired back the next day that he should proceed. So on February 25, 1927, Lindbergh signed the order for his plane.

DESIGNING THE PLANE

With the business portion of his goal complete, Lindbergh turned his attention to what excited and interested him—building his plane and planning his flight. Lindbergh worked with Ryan engineer Donald Hall to design each element of the plane to meet Lindbergh's own high standards and to emphasize efficiency of flight, regardless of the detriment to the pilot's comfort. Lindbergh wrote, "First consideration [is] to efficiency in flight; second, to protection in a crack-up [crash]; third, to pilot comfort."[28] To increase flight efficiency, for example, the gas tank was installed in the nose of the plane, rather than behind the pilot's seat as was usually done. This design obstructed the pilot's forward vision—he would see only the instrument panel in front of him, not the sky. But Lindbergh did not care. His view from the sides of the plane would be sufficient. Additionally, emergency equipment was kept to a minimum. Heavy items that would have been standard, such as an inflatable rubber raft, were excluded.

Lindbergh worked long hours at the factory, at one point staying awake working for thirty-six hours. The Ryan plane builders, a group of enthusiastic young

Lindbergh performs maintenance on his plane, the Spirit of St. Louis, *in 1927.*

men, worked equally long hours. Everyone was motivated to work as fast as possible, as news of competitors' preparations appeared daily in the newspapers.

NAVIGATION

Lindbergh also spent long hours preparing navigational charts for the flight. Since no one had ever flown the course Lindbergh planned, no navigational charts of the area existed for pilots. In his flights around the United States, Lindbergh had frequently used inexpensive railroad maps, tracing roads and landmarks by sight. But a flight over the uncharted Atlantic posed many problems because he would not be able to use landmarks for most of the flight.

Lindbergh flew to San Pedro, California, to a store that carried naval shipping maps of the Atlantic. He bought several and brought them back to Hall's office, making computations with a compass and ruler to figure his route. Because the maps were not made for aviation, he had to estimate many of the figures and came up with a total distance of 3,610 miles for the journey, just within the plane's promised range.

CRASHES AND MISHAPS

In April, as the Ryan Aircraft workers neared completion of construction of the plane, Lindbergh read of the problems and accidents, some of them fatal, which his competitors suffered. On April 16 Com-

mander Byrd's plane, *America*, crashed during its test flight. On April 24 Clarence Chamberlin's plane, *Columbia*, also crash landed during a test flight. Then, two days later Lieutenant Commander Noel Davis and Lieutenant Stanton Wooster were killed while running tests in their plane, *American Legion*. The last news was unnerving to Lindbergh. In his journal, he wrote, "Davis and Wooster killed! My God! Every one of the big multi-engine planes built for the New York–Paris flight has crashed. . . . Four men have lost their lives [including the two who died in the September 1926 crash in Fonck's plane] and three have been injured."[29]

The incidents did not alleviate the urgency of the competition, however. Lindbergh read that Commander Byrd's plane would be repaired by the middle of May and that Captain Nungesser's plane was due to take off by the end of April.

THE *SPIRIT OF ST. LOUIS*

At the end of April 1927 the factory work on Lindbergh's plane was complete. The plane was one of a kind, built specifically to fit Lindbergh and his flight's particular needs. It weighed 2,150 pounds empty and 5,180 pounds when fully loaded with 450 gallons of gasoline, equipment, and its 160-pound pilot. Because of design and instrument improvements, the total cost had risen to fourteen thousand dollars, but even that was less than Lindbergh had raised from his investors, so he was pleased.

There was one final thing to be done, though. The plane needed a name. Harold

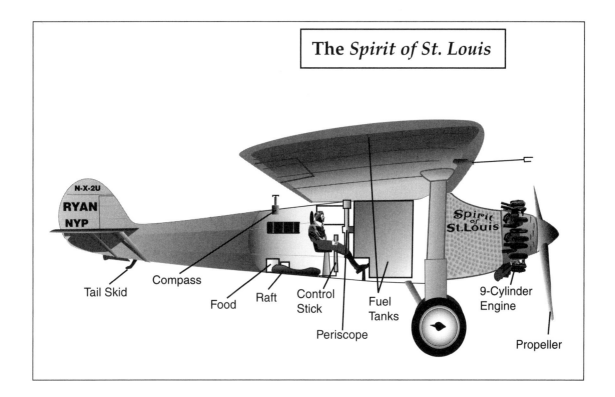

The *Spirit of St. Louis*

Tail Skid
Compass
Food
Raft
Control Stick
Periscope
Fuel Tanks
9-Cylinder Engine
Propeller
N-X-2U
RYAN NYP
Spirit of St. Louis

Bixby, one of Lindbergh's investors, suggested christening the plane the *Spirit of St. Louis* in honor of the investors' home city. Lindbergh agreed, and the name was painted on the fuselage before the plane was towed out of the hangar for its test flights.

TEST FLIGHTS

Lindbergh and the Ryan workers used Dutch Flats, a field in south San Diego, to fly the plane's first test flights. On the morning of April 28, Lindbergh climbed into the lightweight wicker seat in the cockpit and closed the door. He shouted "Contact!" and Ryan's chief mechanic John van der Linde turned the propeller,

successfully starting the motor for the first time. Lindbergh taxied forward and opened the motor's throttle, adding gas to the engine to speed it up, and then the plane took off; it had traveled less than one hundred yards down the runway.

Lindbergh tested the plane dozens of times over the following week. For each flight, more gasoline was loaded into the plane's tanks. The increasing weight made takeoff, handling, and landing more difficult each time. By the time the *Spirit of St. Louis* was tested on May 4 with two-thirds its full load of gasoline, the landing and takeoff were quite rough. The danger of a flight with a full load was apparent. But Lindbergh was satisfied. Although there would be a risk with a fully loaded plane, he accepted it. Time was running out.

WHITE BIRD LOST

On May 8, 1927, it seemed time had indeed run out. While waiting for the weather to clear so he could fly across the United States to New York, Lindbergh read that Nungesser and Coli had taken off from France in the *White Bird* that morning. Assuming they would make it, Lindbergh immediately turned his attention to a transpacific flight instead. "Nungesser and Coli are in the air with full tanks," he wrote in his journal that day. "They're experienced men. They should land in New York tomorrow. I spend most of the day studying charts and data I've assembled for the westward, Pacific flight."[30]

Lindbergh was disappointed, but he wished the men success. When someone tried to console him by saying, "I almost hope they don't make it," Lindbergh angrily retorted, "Don't say that!"[31]

Tragic news came the next day from Paris, however. Nungesser and Coli's plane had not been seen since it left French air space the day before. The pilots were presumed lost or dead. "Only one thing is definite," Lindbergh wrote, "the *White Bird* is down somewhere short of its goal on land or on sea, for time has exhausted its fuel."[32] Neither *White Bird* nor its pilots were seen again.

The disappearance of the French pilots again emphasized to Lindbergh the danger of his plan. But he was resolute. He waited anxiously for the weather over California to clear so that he could leave for New York.

San Diego to New York

On the afternoon of May 10 the weather cleared. Lindbergh packed a small travel bag for the cross-country journey and went to the Ryan factory to say good-bye and thank-you to the workers there. As he left, one worker shouted, "Send us a wire [telegram] when you get to Paris!"[33]

With 250 gallons of gasoline in its tanks, the *Spirit of St. Louis* took off from North Island Naval Station in San Diego at 3:55 P.M., Pacific standard time. Lindbergh was headed for Lambert Field in St. Louis. From there, he would fly to Curtiss Field in New York. As he ascended into the skies above San Diego, he was escorted by two army observation planes and a Ryan monoplane. Together the four planes circled the Ryan Aircraft factory in a salute. Then Lindbergh's plane headed east alone.

He crossed the border of Arizona at sunset and flew through the night. He traveled through the Rocky Mountains at heights of more than twelve thousand feet. The next morning at 8:20 A.M., he landed at Lambert Field, having gone 1,550 miles in fourteen hours and twenty-five minutes. He took off again at 8:13 A.M. the next morning and seven hours later arrived in New York, setting a transcontinental speed record.

The Press

By the time Lindbergh reached New York on May 12, 1927, he was no longer an unknown airmail pilot. The press had picked up on the story of his dangerous and dramatic plans to cross the Atlantic alone. Reporters portrayed Lindbergh as a young underdog competing for the Orteig Prize

---

The *Spirit of St. Louis* Specifications

Wingspan: 46 feet
Length: 27 feet, 8 inches
Height: 9 feet, 10 inches
Weight, empty: 2,150 pounds
Weight, gross: 5,135 pounds
Maximum speed: 129 miles per hour
Flight altitude: 10,000 feet
Range: 4,210 miles
Engine: Wright Whirlwind J-5C, 223 horsepower
Manufacturer: Ryan Airlines Co.

Lindbergh (third from right) poses for a promotional picture with the Spirit of St. Louis, *which he would soon fly across the Atlantic.*

against his two famed and favored contenders, Byrd and Chamberlain.

Upon landing at Curtiss Field, Lindbergh was met by dozens of photographers and reporters clamoring for interviews and photos. Although he was not comfortable with the media attention, he agreed to be photographed and interviewed to publicize his upcoming flight. He felt the attention would benefit aviation and his investors.

Reporters filled the lobby of Lindbergh's hotel, and he spent hours over the next few days talking with them. Lindbergh was charming and friendly, and the reporters were pleased to write about him. They nicknamed him Lucky Lindy, the Flyin' Fool (because he was the only contender to attempt the flight alone), and the Kid.

At first Lindbergh found it exciting to be the center of press attention, but the enjoyment was short-lived. When he read several reporters' inaccurate and fabricated accounts of things he said, it troubled him. "I was shocked by the inaccuracy and sensationalism of many of the articles resulting from my interviews," he wrote. "I found myself quoted as saying things I had neither said nor thought. . . . Contacts with the press became increasingly distasteful to me."[34]

One example of deliberately inaccurate reporting took place when his mother came to see him as he waited in New York. The press asked her and Lindbergh to hug for the cameras. Lindbergh and his mother refused, but the next day papers printed altered photographs of the two embracing. Lindbergh was angry and wrote that such acts undermined his confidence in the press: "I thought it cheaply sentimental and thoroughly dishonest on the part of the papers. . . . I began to realize how much irresponsibility and license

can lurk behind the shining mask called 'freedom of the press.'"[35]

THE WAIT

For nearly a week, Lindbergh and the other pilots waited to take off. The weather over the North Atlantic Ocean remained bad for several days. Lindbergh spent the time tuning up his plane and going over his flight plans. Then, on the evening of May 19, the weather report announced that the skies over the Atlantic were clearing. Lindbergh prepared for a possible takeoff at dawn the next morning. But that night, as he went over his flight plans a final time, Lindbergh suddenly realized he had a problem. The runway at

ONE LAST OBSTACLE

When the construction of Lindbergh's plane was finished, the factory workers prepared to roll it out of its hangar to attach the wing to the fuselage. But, as A. Scott Berg describes in his book Lindbergh, *they discovered they had built the wings too long to fit through the hangar doorway.*

"The next step was to assemble the wing to the fuselage. That first meant getting the two pieces outside the building [hangar]. Not until the workers removed the landing gear on one side of the plane could they pass the fuselage through the great door of the Ryan factory. The wing went less easily. In the constant revising of the plane's design, it had grown ten feet longer than originally planned; and, short of knocking out part of the factory wall, there appeared no way of freeing it from the second-story loft where it had been built. Measuring down to a fraction of an inch, they at last realized that by tilting it, they could slide it out onto the top of an empty [train] boxcar that could be pushed along a railroad [track running] next to the factory. From there the wing was lowered . . . onto a waiting truck."

Curtiss Field was too short for takeoff with his fully loaded plane. The flight in sudden jeopardy, Lindbergh became discouraged. Fortunately, the adjoining Roosevelt Field's runway had been extended by Commander Byrd for the takeoff of his own large trimotor plane. Although he had exclusive rights to use Roosevelt Field, Byrd offered Lindbergh free use of the runway out of a sense of good sportsmanship. Lindbergh gratefully accepted the gesture.

With that worry out of the way, Lindbergh went to bed at midnight, although he did not sleep. He was kept awake all night by dozens of reporters downstairs who were staying up all night in the hotel lobby awaiting his takeoff next morning.

TAKEOFF

As Lindbergh walked onto Roosevelt Field the next morning, he carried only a bag of five sandwiches. Surprised, one reporter asked him if that was all he was taking with him. Lindbergh replied, "Wu-ll, if I get to Paris I won't need any more food, and if I don't, I won't need any either."[36]

Lindbergh's joke pleased the reporters. It also showed his sense of humor about the danger of the flight. He knew that the odds were against his success. There were several things working against him as he climbed into the cockpit of his plane. Despite his careful preparations, for example, when the plane was fully loaded, it was more than one hundred pounds heavier than anticipated. The weather re-

Lindbergh poses with his mother before embarking on his historic transatlantic flight in 1927.

ports were still uncertain. And he had already been awake for twenty-three hours; with a thirty-six-hundred-mile solo flight ahead of him, Lindbergh would not be able to sleep for thirty to forty more hours.

A final problem came just before takeoff. When Lindbergh started the motor to his plane, his mechanic told him the engine was running slower than normal because of the damp weather. That meant that Lindbergh would not have all the power he expected for the already dangerous takeoff. At the end of the runway, telephone wires ran across the field. If he could not get the plane high enough by the end of the runway, he would certainly collide with them and crash. Further, once he got down the runway to a certain point—"the point of no return," he would not have enough time to stop the plane before it crashed, even if he knew the takeoff was failing. Lindbergh sat in his plane weighing the dangers. He recalled his thoughts:

> Suppose I *do* get off the ground—will fog close in and force me back? Suppose the [visibility] drops to zero—I can't fly blind with this overload of fuel. . . . Shall I cut the switch and wait another day for confirmation of good weather? . . . Wind, weather, power, load—gradually these elements stop churning in my mind. It's less a decision of logic than a feeling . . . sitting in the cockpit, in the seconds, minutes long, the conviction surges through me that the wheels *will* leave

the ground, that the wings *will* rise above the wires, that it *is* time to start the flight.[37]

Lindbergh put on his flight helmet and goggles, pushed wads of cotton into his ears to muffle the sound of the motor, and buckled his safety belt. He gave the signal to start the propeller. "Action brings confidence and relief,"[38] he thought. He opened the motor to full throttle and taxied down the runway. Workers pushed the plane to help the engine compensate for the weight and muddy field. As he built up speed, Lindbergh worked the plane's controls to keep it from lifting off until the right moment. "The wrong decision means a crash—probably in flames,"[39] he thought. Soon the plane passed the point of no return. Then it slowly lifted from the ground, rising into the air, clearing the telephone wires at the end of the runway by only twenty feet. The *Spirit of St. Louis* ascended into the air on its way to Paris. It was 7:54 A.M. eastern daylight time, May 20, 1927.

Chapter

4 Fame

Lindbergh's transatlantic flight received unprecedented world attention, and when he successfully landed in France, he became a world hero. But Lindbergh was a private, quiet, reticent young man; his new fame overwhelmed him and permanently altered his life in ways he had never anticipated. Although he was honored by the attention bestowed upon him and used his notoriety to benefit the field of aviation, he was cautious about the decisions he made and became wary of the easy money and celebrity fame offered.

FREEDOM OF FLIGHT

After take-off, Lindbergh navigated his plane out of New York's airspace toward Nova Scotia. Three hours later, the coastline of the United States disappeared from sight behind him. He reduced altitude and flew just 150 feet above the ocean surface, where he knew an air cushion just above the water would give him the smoothest ride. He consulted his navigation charts and used a compass to make sure he was flying the proper course.

His plane on course, Lindbergh settled inside the cockpit, feeling the snug fit of his plane, elated by the freedom he felt out of sight of land. He later wrote, "No man before me had commanded such freedom of movement. I had enough gasoline to fly northward to the Pole, or southward to the Amazon, or to Africa, if I wished to change my course. For me the *Spirit of St. Louis* was a lens focused on the future, a forerunner of mechanisms that would conquer time and space."[40]

FIGHTING FATIGUE

The hours and miles passed slowly, but Lindbergh kept busy, checking his charts, writing in his plane's log, and thinking. His isolated childhood had prepared him for this long flight alone, and he kept his mind engaged and alert by having long conversations with himself. He remembered his past and thought about the possibilities of the future. But by afternoon, Lindbergh felt his fatigue growing. He wrote, "I've lost command of my eyelids. When they start to close, I can't restrain them. They shut, and I shake myself, and lift them with my fingers. I stare at the instruments, wrinkle my forehead muscles tense. Lids close again regardless, stick tight as though with glue."[41]

Lucky Lindy waves from the cockpit minutes before the Spirit of St. Louis *takes off.*

Lindbergh could not afford to fall asleep or lapse into inattention, however. Doing so risked falling off course, getting lost at sea, or wrecking the plane. He tried to keep alert by removing the side window glass of his plane, flying low over the waves and putting his head outside. He felt the cold ocean's spray on his face. He flexed and stretched and stamped his feet. He checked and rechecked instruments. He talked to himself, chiding himself to keep awake: "I've got to find some way to keep alert," he recalled thinking. "There's no alternative but death and failure. *No alternative but death and failure,* I keep repeating, using the thought as a whip on my lagging mind; trying to make my senses realize the importance of what I'm saying."[42]

BATTLING THE STORM

After eight hours in the air Lindbergh looked down and saw land. It was Nova Scotia, the last North American landmark before two thousand miles of ocean opened between him and Europe. The next land he could expect to see was Ireland. For the next fifteen hours of flight he would be out of sight, except for the chance sighting by a ship at sea.

During the first night of the flight, at 10,500 feet Lindbergh encountered a storm that almost turned him back. He felt the storm before he saw it; a chill came into the fuselage. He then put a bare hand outside the window and felt the sting of ice. He aimed his flashlight outside and saw the plane was covered in ice. That meant serious danger. The weight of ice on the plane and wings could affect the ability to fly and cause an accident.

Carefully, he turned the plane around and navigated out of the storm by instinct. When he was under the stars of a clear sky again, he turned east to go around the storm and rejoin what he hoped was his course. Although he escaped the storm, Lindbergh was unsure how far off course he might have gone. He hoped not far.

THE WORLD WATCHED

As Lindbergh battled fatigue and the elements, people all over the globe awaited news about his progress. Newspapers and hourly radio reports tracked Lindbergh's transatlantic flight from its start. In New York people congregated beneath large signs in Times Square awaiting the latest news. For many, the disappearance of *White Bird* during the previous week made the fifteen hours that Lindbergh's plane was out of sight especially anxious and tense.

It seemed the entire world had its mind on Lindbergh that night. All over the United States and Europe, at sporting events, banquets, and gatherings, people spoke with expectation and respect for Lindbergh. The stock exchanges all over the world interrupted their quotations to provide updates. Lloyd's of London, a world-renowned auction house, even issued odds (10 to 3 against) on the chances of Lindbergh successfully making it to Paris.

HALLUCINATIONS AND MIRAGES

As the hours passed, Lindbergh's fatigue worsened and he began to hallucinate. "I saw mirages as real as reality had been," he recalled. "I conversed with ghostly forms riding with me in the fuselage."[43] The ghosts permeated the fabric walls of the plane, coming and going. They spoke to him above the noise of the plane, giving him advice. Later, Lindbergh noted that these ghostly figures would have frightened him in other circumstances, but he was so overtired and felt so disconnected from the world that they did not trouble him. "I'm so far separated from the earthly life I know that I accept whatever circumstances may come,"[44] he thought.

In the next hour of his journey, the sun rose and Lindbergh saw what he believed were islands below him. This concerned him; according to his charts, there should not have been any islands in the vicinity. He wondered how far off course he had traveled in avoiding the storm. He shook himself to make sure he was awake and realized that the islands were mirages. Although he was somewhat relieved, it troubled him because he was concerned that he might not know Europe for certain when he saw it.

After the twenty-seventh hour of his flight, Lindbergh looked down and again saw objects below. This time it was no mirage but a fleet of small fishing boats. Ex-

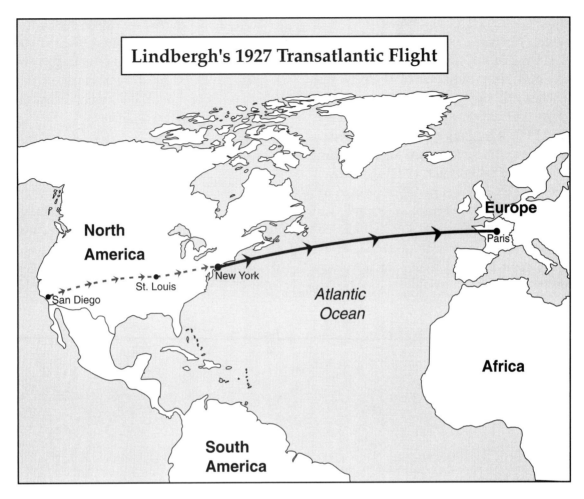

Lindbergh's 1927 Transatlantic Flight

North America

Europe

Paris

San Diego

St. Louis

New York

Atlantic Ocean

Africa

South America

cited, he flew low, within fifty feet of the water, and circled one of the boats. He shouted out the window of his plane, "Which way is Ireland!"[45] He passed the ship several times but got no response. But by his calculations, he was sure that he had at least another two-and-a-half hours before reaching land.

FINAL MILES

Lindbergh continued flying, encountering rain and fog along the way. Then only an

hour later, he saw a coastline fifteen miles to the northeast. Excited, he changed his course and headed for the land. He had reached the southwest coast of Ireland. His fatigue vanished instantly.

As Lindbergh flew over England an hour later, he felt a surge of happiness and optimism. The difficulties of the flight were behind him. The plane, now seventeen hundred pounds lighter after the expenditure of fuel, handled easily. The remaining distance to France was less than that of a mail run from St. Louis to Chicago. As the sun began to set, Lindbergh reached the French coast. Below, people ran out to watch his plane pass overhead. For the first time during the flight, he felt his appetite and took out one of his five sandwiches and ate it.

At 9:52 P.M. Paris's Eiffel Tower came into view. Lindbergh circled the tower in a salute and then searched for the landing field called Le Bourget. Locating the field proved challenging. He looked down trying to find a dark space surrounded by regularly spaced lights, but the only area he could see was surrounded by an erratic pattern of lights. He flew a few more miles looking for the field without success

then returned to that first spot. As he circled more closely, he located the airfield below and realized that the thousands of lights surrounding the field were the headlamps of automobiles stuck in traffic on their way to greet him.

HISTORIC LANDING

Lindbergh steered the *Spirit of St. Louis* toward the airfield. The plane touched down gently and rolled forward to a stop. The time in Paris was 10:24 P.M., Saturday, May 21, 1927. The flight had taken thirty-

The Spirit of St. Louis *touches down at Le Bourget Airfield on May 21, 1927.*

three-and-a-half hours. Lindbergh turned the plane toward the hangars, but a massive crowd—an estimated 100,000 people—gathered at the field and rushed to the plane, cheering and shouting his name. "No sooner had my plane touched the ground," he remembered, "than a human sea swept toward it."[46] Alarmed, he stopped the plane.

Lindbergh then climbed from the cockpit and was jerked into the air by someone in the crowd. The well-wishers carried him around the field for a half hour on their shoulders. Souvenir hunters attacked his plane, tearing pieces of fabric from it. During the onslaught, someone reached inside and stole Lindbergh's log book.

Finally, Lindbergh was rescued from the crowd by two French military pilots who pulled off his helmet and put it on an American reporter to confuse the crowd. The trick worked, and the men escaped with Lindbergh to a car. Meanwhile, French police and military guards were dispatched to the field to protect the plane from further damage.

Hero at Rest

That night the American ambassador to France, Myron T. Herrick, drove Lindbergh away from Le Bourget and through Paris, showing him some of the city sights including the tomb of France's Unknown Soldier, where Lindbergh paid his respects. Herrick then took him to the American embassy where reporters waited. Graciously and briefly, Lindbergh answered a few questions before Herrick dismissed

the press in order to give Lindbergh the chance to rest. Herrick showed Lindbergh to his room, and at 4:15 A.M. Lindbergh went to bed, sleeping for the first time in sixty-three hours. Although Lindbergh did not realize it as he slept, his life had changed forever. In the course of his flight, he had become the most famous man on Earth.

A Global Media Event

On May 21, 1927, all other world news was moved from the front pages in the United States and Europe to make room for headlines about Lindbergh's flight. He became famous overnight. When news arrived in the United States of Lindbergh's successful arrival in Paris, word spread quickly and celebrations broke out in towns and cities all over the country. Cars on the streets and boats in harbors blew their horns. Fire engines sounded their sirens; people on bullhorns drove through city streets announcing the news. Radios played "The Star Spangled Banner" and the French national anthem, "Marseillaise." Similar celebrations broke out in Europe, and adulation and congratulations poured into the American embassy in Paris.

"A New Environment of Life"

When Lindbergh awoke in his room at the embassy on the afternoon of May 22, 1927, it was to the sound of a crowd outside his window chanting and calling his name. Ambassador Herrick suggested

IN THE CROWD

When Charles Lindbergh landed his plane at Le Bourget field near Paris on May 21, 1927, he was greeted by more than one hundred thousand people who charged the field to meet the plane. Julia Richards, a Massachusetts woman on vacation in France with her husband and children, was one of these people. In a letter written a few days after Lindbergh's landing, Richards describes what it was like to be part of the crowd. Her letter was reprinted in an article entitled, "We Saw Him Land," in the May 2002 issue of Smithsonian *magazine.*

"It must have been a quarter past ten when the roar of an aeroplane overhead was distinctly heard above the answering roar of the mob below. It passed, but all about us had distinctly seen the outline of a plane. A few minutes more and we heard it again; it grew in volume and then suddenly, out of the black darkness, there flew a great silver moth—it seemed to me—which glided down the path of light in the middle of the field and was suddenly swallowed up again in the seething, howling mass of humanity that surged towards it from every direction of the compass. One second I was gazing softly down its lighted way; the next I was gazing at a sheer black wall of humanity trying to fight its way up over a six-foot iron fence.

Two seconds later the fence gave way, and the black wave broke and swept forward like the Mississippi floods. . . . [My family] meant to escape then and there, but when we emerged from our protected corner, the fever took possession of us too, and we longed for just one nearer glimpse before we should go. . . . We saw the plane all right. . . . It was moving slowly across the field—being pushed to its hangar we supposed. . . . It was almost abreast of us when to our horror it suddenly turned at right angles and charged straight down upon us! It was a nasty moment; everybody was running in every direction and every third person was trundling a bicycle. . . . [B]efore it [the plane] was finally rescued, ardent souvenir hunters had succeeded in cutting good-sized pieces of cloth out of the wings."

that he say a few words to the crowd. A private man, the thought of exhibiting himself disturbed and embarrassed Lindbergh, but he felt duty bound to comply. The publicity he received was important to his investors and to aviation. Lind-bergh dressed in a suit borrowed from the ambassador and stepped out onto the balcony. There he was greeted by the loud applause and cheers of the thousands of people lining the embassy courtyard and street. Reporters, photographers, and movie camera operators pushed forward to get a better look. Lindbergh smiled and, when the crowd quieted, said three of the few words in French he knew: "Vive [long live] la France!"

Standing before that crowd, Lindbergh realized that his life had changed. "I had entered a new environment of life," he later wrote, "and found myself surrounded by unforeseen opportunities, responsibilities, and problems."[47]

SOCIAL DUTY

Lindbergh had originally planned to spend a few leisurely weeks sightseeing in Europe after landing in Paris. But with his new fame and notoriety, it was obvious that he would not be able to fulfill these plans. Over the next few days, whenever he left the embassy he traveled with a security entourage, and everywhere he went he was greeted by crowds clamoring for his attention. On more than one occasion young women lunged at him to try to steal a kiss.

Even without the crowds Lindbergh's time was no longer his own. Every moment of his days in Europe was spent fulfilling the obligations of his new notoriety. Invitations poured in from European leaders, dignitaries, and royalty. Being the center of so much attention was unnerving and uncomfortable. He attended dinners and gala events, feeling

French fans cheer the famous young aviator. Lindbergh was greeted by enthusiastic crowds throughout Europe.

out of place even though he was the guest of honor.

On May 28 Lindbergh left Paris in the repaired *Spirit of St. Louis* for Brussels, Belgium, and then London, England. Again, he attended ceremonies and dinners dutifully. He gave prepared speeches when necessary but otherwise often sat quietly at his table.

Even though Lindbergh wanted to spend more time in Europe, the United States clamored for his return. He received word that he had been promoted from lieutenant to colonel by the Army Air Reserve Corps, and President Calvin Coolidge sent the United States Navy cruiser *Memphis* to France to bring Colonel Lindbergh and his plane home.

Symbol of Aviation

Lindbergh arrived in America on June 10, 1927, to enormous celebrations in his honor. He was greeted by unprecedented crowds in Washington, D.C. And as he rode through the streets of New York, more than four million people crowded the sidewalks to greet him.

Lindbergh understood that the world assigned special importance to him. "I found myself symbolizing aviation,"[48] he recalled. The responsibility of this position led him to consider how he might use his notoriety to benefit aviation.

One of his first acts was to embark on a forty-eight-state goodwill tour. He flew from one state to the next making speeches and receiving honors and well-wishes from people all over the country.

Lindbergh later wrote that the tour gave him a unique perspective on America.

> The tour let me know my country as no man had ever known it before. . . . I landed in every state in the union, spoke to scores of cities, dropped messages on still more. I inspected sites for airports, talked to engineers and politicians, and tried to convince everyone who would listen that aviation had a brilliant future, in which America should lead.[49]

Ambassador of the Air

In fall 1927, after returning from his American tour, Lindbergh received an invitation from Dwight Morrow, the American ambassador in Mexico, to fly the *Spirit of St. Louis* to Mexico City. Morrow hoped the visit would act as a goodwill gesture to improve relations between the United States and its neighboring country to the south. Lindbergh accepted the offer and decided that he would fly nonstop from Washington, D.C., to Mexico City, symbolically joining the two nations' capitals with his flight. He would then continue to Central and South America as an unofficial ambassador and to encourage interest in the possibilities of trans-American aviation.

On December 13, 1927, at 12:22 P.M., Lindbergh took off in the *Spirit of St. Louis* from Washington, D.C. The 2,100-mile flight took twenty-seven hours and eighteen minutes. He touched down at 3:40 P.M. at Mexico City's Valbuena Field where he was greeted by large, enthusiastic crowds.

Crowds throng a ticker-tape parade greeting Lindbergh on his return to New York.

After six days in Mexico City, Lindbergh took off again. Ultimately, he completed a six-week tour of fourteen Latin American countries. He completed the journey in February 1928 and then returned to St. Louis, Missouri. After this tour Lindbergh made one last flight in the *Spirit of St. Louis*, flying from St. Louis to Washington, D.C. Then, on April 30, 1928, he retired the aircraft, turning it over to the Smithsonian Institution. The plane was placed on permanent exhibition at the Smithsonian along with flight pioneers Orville and Wilbur Wright's plane, *Flyer*.

AIRLINE CONSULTANT

After retiring the *Spirit of St. Louis*, Lindbergh considered his career options.

Almost anything was possible. He had offers of all kinds, from companies wanting him to sponsor their products to aircraft and airline companies wanting him to become an executive. He was even offered large sums of money to appear in movies and traveling live entertainment shows called vaudeville. All told, he was offered enough money to live the rest of his life without working again.

But Lindbergh was not interested in fame and easy money. To him, celebrity without purpose was pointless. More than anything, he wanted to contribute to the growth of aviation, particularly commercial aviation. To this end, in late 1927 and early 1928, he became a technical adviser and consultant for two new airlines, Transcontinental Air Transport (TAT) and Pan American Airways. With Lindbergh's help, TAT established the first commercial transcontinental air routes in America, and Pan American established the first intercontinental routes among North, Central, and South America. Through the late 1920s and early 1930s, Lindbergh surveyed and chose new routes, helped decide where to build airports, and helped choose what kinds of planes would be best for commercial air travel.

ANNE

This professional life satisfied Lindbergh, and he felt the only part of his life lacking was a family. But Lindbergh, who was one of the most accomplished and famous young men in the world, had never even had a girlfriend. Until the completion of his transatlantic trip, he had not had the interest or opportunity to pursue a rela-

---

ROCKET MAN

In November 1929 Lindbergh met with a Clark University research physicist named Robert H. Goddard. Goddard did research into early rockets and suggested the possibility of creating a rocket with sufficient power to escape Earth's gravity and travel into space. In his book Autobiography of Values, *Lindbergh recalls his response to his first meeting with Goddard.*

"I am sure Professor Goddard had no idea how his words set my mind spinning. A flight to the moon [was] theoretically possible! An altitude of one hundred miles predictable within a few more years! Then space was to be an extension of, not a limit to, the works of man. The rocket, like the wheel, the hull, and the wing, would throw back old horizons. . . . Maybe a man would learn how to travel faster than the speed of light. Impossible? Who dared now, to say anything was impossible!"

---

tionship. He was also aware that because of his celebrity, it would be difficult to date. He wrote:

> I had always taken for granted that someday I would marry and have a family of my own, but I had not thought much about it. In fact, I had never been interested enough in any girl to ask her on a date. . . . [After the transatlantic flight], [n]ewspapers had reported me engaged to at least a dozen women, several of whom I had never seen. It was quite clear that any relationships I had with women would be exaggerated and complicated by the attention of the press. Nevertheless, I decided it was time to meet girls.[50]

The woman he chose was Anne Morrow, the twenty-one-year-old daughter of the American ambassador to Mexico. Lindbergh had stayed a week at the ambassador's during the previous winter and had met the shy and quiet young woman who spent more time reading books and writing in her diary than socializing. During Lindbergh's stay, Morrow developed a crush on Lindbergh but had not spoken much to him. After Lindbergh left Mexico, she presumed that he had not noticed her. He had, though. In October 1928 he telephoned her at the Morrow family home in Englewood, New Jersey, to ask her on a date to take her flying. Morrow agreed.

The first date went well. The couple got along and Morrow loved flying. "Can't describe it," she wrote, "it was too glorious."[51]

A QUICK COURTSHIP, A SECRET WEDDING

Lindbergh and Morrow went on a second date a few days later. This time, they took a drive through New Jersey. During that date, Lindbergh proposed marriage and Morrow accepted.

Although Lindbergh tried to keep the relationship a secret, the press found out that he was seeing someone. Reporters followed him everywhere trying to find out the identity of the woman. Discovering that it was one of the Morrow household, the press made an assumption and ran stories that Lindbergh was engaged to Anne's older sister Elizabeth Morrow.

Although Anne Morrow understood the need for privacy, she was unaccustomed to the secrecy. Lindbergh cautioned her, however, that the press had no respect for privacy and that she had to be very careful about her telephone calls and correspondence. Anne Morrow wrote,

> I was warned by my husband-to-be, an intensely private person who was determined to keep intact this most private of all relationships: 'Never say anything you wouldn't want shouted from the housetops, and never write anything you would mind seeing on the front page of a newspaper.'[52]

The day of their wedding, May 27, 1929, reporters camped out in front of the Morrow home, as they had done since discovering that Lindbergh was dating one of the Morrows. Dwight Morrow and his

Lindbergh is pictured with his wife, Anne Morrow. She shared his love of flying.

wife informally invited family and close friends over for lunch. No one outside the immediate family (other than the pastor and the wedding-dress maker) knew that the guests were there to witness a wedding. The wedding was successfully kept secret until the couple had already left for their honeymoon.

A Public Life

From the beginning of their marriage, Charles and Anne Lindbergh were followed everywhere by reporters and photographers. On their honeymoon, the Lindberghs sailed a motorboat up the New England coast from Massachussets

The First Meeting

In December 1927, twenty-one-year-old Anne Morrow, the daughter of the American ambassador in Mexico, met Charles Lindbergh at a party in her home. In her diary, published in her book Bring Me a Unicorn: Diaries and Letters, 1922–1928, *Morrow describes her first impressions of her future husband.*

"I saw standing against [a] great stone pillar . . . a tall, slim boy in evening dress—so much slimmer, so much taller, so much more poised than I expected. A very refined face, not at all like those grinning 'Lindy' pictures—a firm mouth, clear, straight blue eyes, fair hair, and nice color. I went down the [receiving] line, very confused and overwhelmed by it all. He did not smile—just bowed and shook hands. . . . [Later, after the party he spoke. He was] terribly shy—looked straight ahead and talked in short direct sentences which came out abruptly and clipped. You could not meet his sentences: they were statements of fact, presented with such honest directness; not trying to please. . . . It was amazing—breath-taking. I could not speak."

to Maine. They were discovered several times by the media and had to keep sailing north to get away from reporters. At one point during the trip, a reporter relentlessly circled the Lindbergs' boat for eight hours, trying to get photographs of the couple. Lindbergh had to speed off toward the open sea to escape the reporter.

When the couple returned to New Jersey, Charles and Anne could not go out in public without being surrounded by the press. The only place they could be alone was in the air, so they spent increasing amounts of time flying. Lindbergh gave his wife flying lessons and she became a good pilot. But on the ground, they used assumed names when staying in hotels and wore disguises to enjoy simple outings.

The media attention only increased when in fall 1929 the press discovered that Anne Lindbergh was pregnant. However, when the child, Charles Augustus Lindbergh Jr., was born on June 22, 1930, the Lindberghs did not publicly announce the birth. Lindbergh also refused to give interviews or to allow photographers to take pictures of the baby. Several papers, frustrated by the Lindberghs' refusal to give news or photos of the child, printed stories that the baby was deformed or had been stillborn. This made Lindbergh furious. He began keeping a list of journalists and newspapers who printed such rumors and vowed never to cooperate with them again.

Hoping to appease the press and reduce the amount of media harassment his new family received, Lindbergh decided

Anne Lindbergh spends a quiet moment with her son. The attention that greeted his birth overwhelmed the Lindberghs.

to release a photograph of the baby to the press. He took and developed the photo himself and distributed it to newspapers, except those on his blacklist. Nonetheless, within a day every newspaper in the world had a copy of the picture.

In the five years since his historic flight, Lindbergh had grown increasingly aggravated and weary of the attention of the press and fans. As he and his wife began their new life as parents, Lindbergh was determined to protect his child from the media and to raise him in as normal a family environment as possible. Ultimately, however, he would fail.

5 Tragedy and Danger

During the early 1930s Lindbergh's fame continued to be a burden. Now married, Lindbergh wanted to embark on what he considered a normal life of family and work, but the attention of the press and fans made such a "normal" existence impossible. As Lindbergh tried to keep his family away from publicity, the press refused to relent, causing a constant struggle between Lindbergh's desire for privacy and the press's determination to keep him in the public eye. And it was this struggle, Lindbergh believed, that eventually led to the worst tragedy of his life.

THE FLYING COUPLE

Since Lindbergh's 1927 transatlantic flight, various pilots had made several important air expeditions to regions of the Pacific, and as Lindbergh read about them, he felt restless and eager to participate in the explorations. Thus, in spring 1931, even though Charles Jr. was still just a baby, Lindbergh decided that he and Anne should take an air expedition to China and Japan. Lindbergh's upbringing led him to believe that children should be

raised to be independent and that some degree of separation was healthy, even at an early age. To this end, Lindbergh decided that he and his wife should leave Charles Jr. in the care of Anne's family and the Lindbergh's new family nurse, Betty Gow, and take a several-month trip, beginning that summer.

Although Anne was content to take care of their child and stay close to home, she was also eager to take the trip with her husband during which they would survey possible air routes from America to Asia. In her diary, she wrote, "I would have been content to stay home and do nothing else but care for my baby. . . . But there were those survey flights that lured us to more adventures. I went on them proudly, taking my place as crew member."[53]

Charles Lindbergh's flight plan called for him and Anne to fly north from New York over the Arctic, then east to the coastlines of China and Japan. For the trip Lindbergh modified a monoplane he had bought the previous year, attaching flotation devices called pontoons to replace the landing gear. That way, the plane could land on the ocean and other waterways. Additionally, for the first time in his

The Lindberghs flew over the Arctic to the Far East in 1931. They are pictured here in their monoplane, which Lindbergh fitted with pontoons.

flying career, Lindbergh decided to carry a long-range communications radio on the flight. In years past, he had not used radios because they were unreliable and heavy. But by 1931 the devices were lighter weight and more reliable, so he decided to take one along. He taught Anne how to use the radio and assigned her the job of being radio operator and navigator, as well as copilot.

RESCUE MISSIONS

The Lindberghs left in July 1931 and spent three months traveling to Canada, Alaska, Russia, Japan, and China. Although Anne experienced homesickness and missed her baby, for the most part, she and her husband enjoyed the time alone together. They were both especially glad to get away from the media and the fans.

When they reached China in September 1931, the Lindberghs volunteered to help the National Flood Relief Commission, an organization providing food and medical aid to victims of floods along China's overflowing Yangtze River. The floods had left millions of people homeless, and the Lindberghs' plane was particularly useful because it could fly supplies into remote areas. Lindbergh flew several rescue flights around the country, sometimes with Anne and sometimes carrying medical doctors. For their rescue efforts, the Chinese government awarded the Lindberghs the country's National Medal.

FAMILY MAN

On October 5, 1931, while the Lindberghs were still in China, Anne received a telegram carrying bad news. Her father, Am-

DELIVERING AID

In 1931, while in China, Lindbergh helped with rescue efforts for flood victims. He used a pontoon plane, a modified plane that can land on water, to fly medical supplies and food to regions otherwise unreachable. It was a dangerous undertaking, and in Autobiography of Values *he describes an incident when his plane nearly capsized.*

"I had two doctors, one American, the other Chinese, on board. . . . We landed . . . near the center of a huge flooded district. The nearest dry land was twenty-five miles south.

A sampan [small boat] sculled up to us. The Chinese doctor hired it to take him and the packages of [medicine] to a city gate. . . . Several minutes passed before the bargaining was completed. By that time dozens of sampans had surrounded us and dozens more were converging from all directions. The people were starving. . . . They thought the packages we brought contained food. . . .

Before long the sampans were jammed beam to beam. Together they must have formed an acre or two. Thin ragged figures began moving toward us, jumping and crawling from boat to boat. . . . A fight started over the package. . . . I saw countless hands hanging on to the wings and tail of our plane. The sterns of our pontoons were already pushed underwater by the weight of human bodies.

Under my parachute I had wedged a . . . revolver . . . . Our plane would sink. We might not get out alive. . . . I whipped my gun [out and pointed it at the crowd]. The surge forward ended. . . . I turned back quickly, firing into the air. . . . Hands let go the wings and tail. Sampans began to shove away. We pulled the Chinese doctor back on board, hoisted anchor, and took off."

---

bassador Dwight Morrow, had died unexpectedly from a stroke. Thus, the Lindberghs returned to the United States in early November to attend the funeral in New Jersey.

Anne mourned her father but was happy to be reunited with her child. Charles Jr., now almost sixteen months old, did not recognize his parents at first, but soon warmed to them. Anne had observed that her husband had been distant with the child before they left for their journey, but when they returned, Anne wrote to her mother-in-law that Charles seemed to have settled in and now felt comfortable and happy as a father:

It is good to be home—and oh, the baby! He is a boy, a strong independent boy swaggering around on his firm little legs. He did not know us but was not afraid of us—not at *all* afraid of C. [Charles Lindbergh], which pleased C. tremendously. He began to take such an interest in the baby—playing with him, spoiling him by giving him cornflakes and toast and sugar and jam off his plate in the morning and tossing him up in the air. After he'd done that once or twice the boy came toward him with outstretched arms.[54]

In February 1932 Charles Lindbergh turned 30. For the first time in his life, he enjoyed the seclusion and quiet of home life. Lindbergh spent evenings with his family, reading and listening to music. For the first few months after his and Anne's return, the young family lived in Englewood with the Morrows. But they were awaiting the completion of a new house near the town of Hopewell, New Jersey. The family was happy and together, and, unbeknownst to the press, Anne Lindbergh was pregnant again.

KIDNAPPED!

By late February the Lindberghs' new house was finished. Located on 425 acres in New Jersey's Sourland Mountains, the house was secluded and difficult to find. It was a two-story, ten-room house complete with servants' quarters and set back from a quiet road. The Lindberghs planned to move into the house in March, but they visited on weekends. The press and public also began spending time there.

Reporters and fans waited for a glimpse of the famous couple and their child. This frustrated Lindbergh. He and his family could not seem to escape from the public eye.

On the last weekend in February 1932 the family stayed at the Hopewell house as usual. Charles, Anne, and Charles Jr. had all caught colds, and the Lindberghs decided to remain at the house for a few more days rather than travel back to Englewood. They thought it would be better for the baby to stay inside and warm rather than travel in the winter cold back to the Morrows' home. Charles Jr.'s nurse, Betty Gow, came to the house to help Anne care for her son.

Then, on the evening of March 1, 1932, after the child was put to bed, someone climbed a ladder to his bedroom and kidnapped him while Charles, Anne, and Betty Gow were downstairs. Years later, Lindbergh would recall the events of that night in his memoirs. He wrote,

> I had been sitting in the parlor with my wife. Outside the wind blew and the night was black. . . . I went upstairs to the child's nursery, opened the door, and immediately noticed a lifted window. A strange-looking envelope lay on the sill. I looked at the crib. It was empty. I ran downstairs, grabbed my rifle, and went into the night, first to the nursery end of the house. Under the lifted window I saw a ladder, and saw that it was broken. Obviously it had collapsed as the kidnapper descended. . . .
>
> I realized there was no use going into the woods or trying to follow along the roads. The night was too dark and

Charles Jr., shown here at age one, was kidnapped from the Lindberghs' New Jersey home in 1932.

stormy to see or hear anything. I returned to the house and put in an emergency call to the State Police.[55]

When the police arrived, they discovered a ransom note and more evidence of an intruder, including footprints leading away from the house and a chisel, which they presumed had been used to pry open the window shutters. The ransom note, crudely written, demanded money, warned against notifying the police, and assured the Lindberghs that the child would be returned safely. It read,

Dear Sir!

Have 50,000 $ redy 25000 $ in 20 $ bills 15000 $ in 10 $ bills and 10000 $ in 5 $ bills. After 2–4 days we will inform you were to deliver the Mony.

We warn you for making anyding public or for notify the Polise the child is in gut [good] care.[56]

MANHUNT

Police quickly established roadblocks around the state, searched cars, awakened and questioned the Lindberghs' neighbors. Numerous police officers assembled at the house along with carloads of reporters and photographers who, Lindbergh wrote, "established their usual interference and confusion."[57]

Immediately, the largest nationwide manhunt up to that time was launched to search for the Lindberghs' baby. Although he had worked hard to keep images of his

THE WORLD'S NIGHTMARE

The kidnapping of Charles Lindbergh Jr. was a well-publicized event that disturbed many people all over the world. In his biography Lindbergh, *A. Scott Berg describes the wide-ranging effect the event had.*

"The Lindbergh kidnapping affected every child and parent in America. . . . For several generations the Lindbergh kidnapping became children's first cautionary tale. They were told never to talk to strangers, and any adults in the vicinity of schoolyards were stopped and questioned. . . .

[Famed mystery writer] Agatha Christie herself was inspired to capture some of the hysteria created by this case in her classic thriller *Murder on the Orient Express*. [Author and illustrator] Maurice Sendak, a poor boy in Brooklyn, was so traumatized by the event that he admitted to having spent a lifetime trying to exorcise [get rid of] his fears through macabre [gruesome] children's books. The Lindbergh case inspired sculptor Isamu Noguchi to create his only 'strictly industrial design,' the 'Radio Nurse' [the predecessor of the modern-day baby monitor]—an intercom that served as 'a device for listening in to other rooms within a house, as a precaution against kidnapping.'"

child from circulating in the press, after the kidnapping Charles Lindbergh released still and motion pictures of Charles Jr. to the news media. He hoped the exposure would hamper the kidnapper's ability to keep the child hidden. The boy's description was also transmitted all over the country via newspaper, radios, and police bulletins.

At Hopewell, Lindbergh ordered the conversion of the family home into an auxiliary police station. The house became headquarters for the investigation. Radio equipment, mattresses, and food were brought in for the dozens of police officers helping the search and investigation.

Because of their fame, the Lindberghs received unprecedented assistance from the government. The investigation was headed by the highest-ranking official in the New Jersey police, superintendant Colonel H. Norman Schwarzkopf. Further, U.S. president Herbert Hoover offered any help his administration could provide. The FBI began tapping the phones of underworld figures who might be involved with kidnapping. In addition, the Secret Service, the Internal Revenue Service, the Postal Inspection Service, and other government agencies did whatever they could to help with the investigation, sharing information and assisting the New Jersey police with any clues possible.

PUBLIC SUPPORT

Public support was also strong. Clubs and organizations all over the nation, including the Boy Scouts, women's organizations, and thousands of private citizens,

The New Jersey police distributed this poster to hundreds of other police departments in hopes of encouraging public help in finding Charles Jr.'s kidnapper.

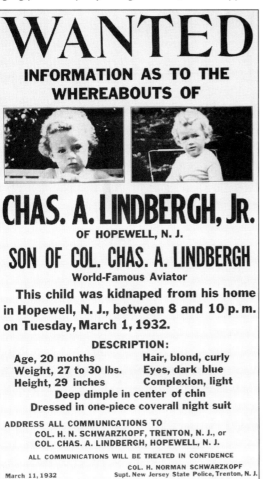

searched the cities and countryside for Charles Jr. The Lindberghs also received an enormous outpouring of international sympathy. Foreign dignitaries, world leaders, and citizens from many countries sent telegrams and letters. And even notorious Chicago gangster Al Capone offered his condolences and a ten-thousand-dollar reward for information leading to the recovery of Charles Jr.

With all the support and offers of help came an extraordinary amount of mail. Three to four thousand pieces of mail came each day. Most of the letters were well intentioned, but a good portion were also fake kidnapping claims, prank letters, accounts of psychic premonitions or dreams, and other unnerving attempts to extort money from the family. Some people even offered their own children to the Lindberghs as a substitute. With the help of police officers, the Lindberghs opened and read every letter, hoping for contact from the kidnappers and any clues or leads other individuals might offer.

The motive for the kidnapping was obvious, both to police and to the Lindberghs. In 1932 the United States was immersed in a severe economic depression. More than thirteen million people were out of work, and many people tried to find a way to alleviate their hardships. Some turned to crime, and kidnapping of the wealthy was one of the most prevalent crimes during those years. With his prize money, consulting income, and other ventures, Charles Lindbergh was by many Americans' standards a wealthy man, and his personal life was so prevalent in the media, his family had become a target for kidnappers.

Lindbergh was willing to pay the kidnappers' ransom in exchange for his son. His main concern was his son's well-being, and he was willing to do whatever was necessary to recover his child.

NEGOTIATIONS

Over the following month and a half, Lindbergh became increasingly involved in the investigation of his child's kidnapping and in the negotiations with the kidnappers. He was worried and concerned, but his wife observed that he also seemed excited by the investigation. She wrote, "The first two days [after the kidnapping] he looked like a desperate man—I could not speak to him. I was afraid to. But these last two days he is quite himself, only stimulated more than usual. . . . He is tireless working [with the police], but he seems very buoyant and alive."[58]

Lindbergh worked closely with New Jersey state police. He insisted on following every lead and spoke to anyone who claimed to have information about his son. He also made all decisions regarding how ransom negotiations would be handled. Because of his notoriety and celebrity, the police allowed Lindbergh to do these things, but his inexpertness in police work actually proved detrimental to the investigation.

In his desperation to retrieve his son, Lindbergh made several decisions many considered ill-advised. For instance, he decided to contact underworld figures, such as an ex-convict named Gaston Means who claimed to know one of the kidnap-

pers from prison. Lindbergh paid Means for information he hoped would lead to the return of his son. The information, however, turned out to be fraudulent. Additionally, Lindbergh appointed John F. Condon, a seventy-one-year-old retired teacher, to serve as a liaison between the Lindberghs and the kidnappers. Lindbergh hoped that using a go-between would make the kidnappers feel more secure during negotiations, thereby ensuring his child's safety. The police advised Lindbergh against hiring Condon because they did not trust him, but Lindbergh hired Condon anyway.

Condon did arrange a night ransom drop with the kidnappers. On the evening of April 9, 1932, he went to St. Raymond's Cemetery in the Bronx, a district of New York City, and gave fifty thousand dollars to a man with a German accent. In exchange Condon received a note telling Lindbergh, who was waiting in a nearby car, where to find his child. The note said that the child was on a boat in the waters off Massachusetts.

TRAGEDY

The note proved to be false, however. Lindbergh and the police spent hours searching for the boat but never found it. Still Lindbergh refused to give up the search. Not knowing what else to do, he continued flying over the waters around Massachussetts for several days, hoping to find his son. Then, a month later, on May 12, 1932, two men driving near the Lindberghs' house in Hopewell came upon a child's body half buried in the bushes near the road. It was Charles Jr. Evidence showed that the child had been there since the night of the kidnapping. He had died from a blow to his skull, possibly from a fall or a blunt instrument.

The Lindberghs were distraught over the death of their child, and each showed grief in a different way. Anne broke down. For days she found it impossible to speak without crying. Charles Lindbergh, however, was calm. He insisted on going to the morgue to identify his child's body even though the identity had already been established by Betty Gow. He examined the boy's toes and teeth and then left the room in silence. Outside the morgue Lindbergh confirmed the identification. "I am perfectly satisfied that is my child," he said. Years later, his daughter Reeve Lindbergh said that such a seemingly emotionless reaction was characteristic of her father. "He wouldn't be able to dissolve into grief or weep and wail or even talk about it. But he could examine, carefully and clinically and that was his strength—some people say it was his weakness, but it's the way he got through his life."[59]

Lindbergh also tried to comfort his wife. He assured her that Charles Jr. had died either during or very soon after his abduction. None of their efforts to rescue the boy could have saved him, and, more important, he would not have had the chance to be frightened or to suffer for long. Anne Lindbergh wrote, "[Charles] spoke so beautifully and calmly about death that it gave me great courage. . . . [Charles Jr.] was such a gay, lordly, as-

sured little boy and had lived always loved and a king in our hearts."[60]

The police investigation into the kidnapping and murder of Charles Jr. continued from the Lindberghs' house. Lindbergh continued to participate, finding it a therapeutic distraction from his grief.

REBUILDING

Despite the ongoing investigation, Charles Lindbergh insisted that he and Anne rebuild their lives. The death of their child would stay with both of them for the rest of their lives, but they had another child on the way to think of. The couple did not return to their home in Hopewell. That house had become linked in their minds with tragedy. It was also attracting more visitors and souvenir hunters than ever. Instead, they moved back into the Morrow home in Engelwood, and Anne focused her energies on their baby.

Not wanting to attract further media attention, the Lindberghs did not hold a funeral for Charles Jr. Instead, they chose to have the boy cremated. On August 15 Lindbergh took off from a New Jersey airfield with his son's ashes. The press met him at the airfield wanting to know his destination, but he kept the journey's purpose a secret. He flew several miles out over the Atlantic Ocean and scattered the ashes.

That night Anne went into labor and early the next morning gave birth to the Lindbergh's second son, whom they named Jon. After the couple brought the baby home, Lindbergh enlisted the help of state troopers and armed guards to patrol the

The Lindbergh's second son, Jon. Shortly after Jon's birth, Lindbergh hired armed guards to protect the family.

grounds of the Morrow home. He also bought a German shepherd and trained it to escort and protect Anne and Jon.

CONTINUED DANGER

Despite these precautions, Lindbergh did not feel that his family was safe. During the first few years of Jon's life, the Lindberghs received hundreds of letters threatening to kidnap him. Intruders came onto the grounds at the Morrow home,

and one night Lindbergh and Anne were chased through traffic by a car carrying four men.

Additionally, Lindbergh and his family continued to be hounded by the press. He believed that the relentless attention of the press, particularly the American press, was responsible for his son's kidnapping and murder, and as time passed, Lindbergh grew more and more disgusted and angry with the media. "As if fanatics and gangsters . . . did not create enough problems for us to contend with, the press itself confronted us with alarming and uncontrollable acts, the most serious of which related to our second son,"[61] he wrote.

Despite pleas by the Lindberghs and many others sympathetic to the family's situation, reporters and photographers continued to hound Lindbergh and his family. When Jon was three, for example, the Lindberghs sent him to nursery school. One day Charles Lindbergh received an emergency phone call from the school saying that a suspicious truck with men in the rear had been parked outside the school at recess. Lindbergh notified the police who stopped the truck as it fled from the school. Inside the truck, police found media photographers who had been trying to get a photo of Jon.

TRIAL OF THE CENTURY

The press attention got worse when, on September 19, 1934, police arrested Bruno Richard Hauptmann, a German-born carpenter living in the Bronx, as a suspect in the kidnapping and murder of Charles

Lindbergh Jr. Police had tracked down Hauptmann through serial numbers on the ransom money Lindbergh had paid in 1932. After much investigation and preparation, on January 2, 1935, the State of New Jersey put Hauptmann on trial for the kidnapping and murder of the Lindbergh baby.

Since Lindbergh's 1927 transatlantic flight, few events had drawn so much public attention. The trial became a media event and a public spectacle. Thousands of members of the press and public, even novelists, movie stars, and members of high society, descended on Flemington, the town where the trial was held, and clamored for seats in the courtroom. The trial was front-page news in major newspapers throughout America for the duration of the month-long trial. In fact, the attention was so great that it was called the "trial of the century" by the media. As one newsreel said, "A quiet town and an old fashioned courthouse turned into a bedlam [chaotic] carnival."[62] Indeed, it seemed as if a carnival were in town. People came from all over the country to be entertained by the trial. Restaurateurs renamed their menus along the theme of the trial and peddlers in the streets sold toy replicas of the ladder found at the scene of the kidnapping.

Charles Lindbergh also attended every day of the trial. He listened quietly and without expression to the presentation of evidence. Both he and Anne took the stand to give their accounts of the events on the night of the kidnapping.

Throughout the trial, Hauptmann maintained his innocence. He claimed that the

PLEA FOR PRIVACY

After their second child, Jon, was born, the Lindberghs feared for his safety. Charles Lindbergh, who laid much blame on the press for the kidnapping of his first child, released an unsuccessful plea to the press. The plea, published in Barry Denenberg's book An American Hero: The True Story of Charles Lindbergh *asks reporters and photographers to allow Jon Lindbergh a normal life out of the spotlight.*

"Mrs. Lindbergh and I have made our home in New Jersey. It is natural that we should wish to continue to live here near our friends and interests. Obviously, however, it is impossible for us to subject the life of our second son to the publicity which we feel was in large measure responsible for the death of our first. We feel that our children have the right to grow up normally with other children. Continued publicity will make this impossible. I am appealing to the Press to permit our children to live the lives of normal Americans."

money found had been given to him by a friend who was no longer in the country and that he had been at work the day of the kidnapping. But his alibi did not hold up; his employer said he had not been at work that day. Further, there was no evidence of the existence of the friend whom he claimed had given him the money.

After eleven hours of deliberation, the jury found Hauptmann guilty of kidnapping and murder. The judge sentenced him to death. After several unsuccessful

TRACKING THE KILLER

The hunt for the criminals behind the kidnapping and murder of the Lindbergh baby lasted more than three years. Police followed hundreds of leads, but the lead that caught Bruno Richard Hauptmann involved tracing ransom money.

When Lindbergh put together the fifty thousand dollars in ransom money to pay the kidnappers, he used gold certificates, which had been the standard U.S. currency since 1900. The bills looked much like modern currency except they were emblazoned with a gold seal. In 1933 the government was in the process of changing the U.S. monetary system from gold certificates to dollars and on April 3—six days before the ransom drop—the U.S. Treasury began calling in gold certificates. This was a break for police because it meant the certificates were easier to spot than standard bills. The police also recorded all of the serial numbers of the bills and provided a list of the serial numbers to banks. In the months following the ransom payment, banks all over the country checked gold certificates against the list and reported any matches to the police.

In September 1934 police followed a lead from one such match found by a teller in a Bronx, New York, bank. On the bill someone had written what police thought was a license plate number, and from this clue police theorized that the bill had been used at a local gas station. The bank where the bill was found was a depository for a service station nearby, and police questioned the manager who recognized the bill and remembered the customer who had given it to him. The manager had spoken to the man, a dark-haired man with a German accent. When the manager had commented about the rarity of the gold certificate, the man had boasted that he had a hundred more like them at home.

Police felt the man was a potential suspect and used the license number written on the certificate to find that the car was registered to Bruno Richard Hauptmann, a German-born carpenter living in the Bronx. Police went to the address under which the car was registered. They confronted Hauptmann with their suspicions and searched his house. There, police found more than fourteen thousand dollars in ransom money hidden in Hauptmann's garage. Furthermore, Hauptmann had no alibi for the night of March 1, 1932, when the Lindbergh baby had been kidnapped. Satisfied they had a strong suspect, police arrested Hauptmann.

A mock lunch menu, reworded during the Hauptmann trial, greets reporters in Flemington in 1935.

appeals, Hauptmann was executed in April 1936.

LEAVING HOME

Finally, the ordeal was over. But after three years of relentless press attention and threats to his family, Charles Lindbergh felt he could not keep his family safe in America. Thus, he decided to leave the country with his wife and son. Lindbergh said, "I decided to take my family abroad until conditions in my own country changed enough to let me establish a reasonably safe and happy home for them."[63] On December 21, 1935, the Lindberghs secretly left America for England by boat. The family traveled on a freighter ship rather than a passenger ship so as to reduce the risk of being discovered.

6 Controversy

The years leading up to and during World War II were difficult and challenging for Charles Lindbergh. Because of his open admiration for the Germans, his outspoken opposition to America's intervention in the war, and his controversial speeches and articles, Lindbergh's public image suffered during the late 1930s and early 1940s, and he lost many friends and associates.

A FRESH START

After landing in Liverpool, England, on December 30, 1935, the Lindberghs spent time sightseeing in London and then toured the English countryside looking for a new place to live. After several weeks of unsuccessful house hunting, they leased a cottage called Long Barn in Kent, a town twenty-five miles southeast of London.

Charles and Anne Lindbergh saw the move as a chance at a fresh start. At first the British media were almost as invasive as the American media had been, but interest about the family quickly tapered off. As they settled into their new home and a relatively less public life, the Lind-

berghs felt safe for the first time since Charles Jr.'s kidnapping. And for the first time since they met, they were able to go out in public without being troubled by the media or overeager fans.

GERMANY

In England Lindbergh continued to work as a consultant for TAT (which changed its name to Trans World Airlines or TWA in the early 1930s) and Pan American. He advised the companies on developments in aviation in Europe. To gather information, he visited aircraft manufacturers and airfields all over England and France to learn about the state of European aviation. He was appalled by much of what he saw. These countries, which had been cultural and world leaders in the recent past, were years behind America in aviation science.

In May 1936 the military adviser to the American embassy in Berlin asked Lindbergh to visit Germany and help assess the development and potential danger of German leader Adolf Hitler's buildup of the *Luftwaffe*, the German Air Force. In 1935 Hitler had violated the Versailles

Treaty, the armistice that ended World War I, by creating the *Luftwaffe*. Having started and lost the First World War, Germany had been forced to dismantle its air force as part of the armistice agreement. Hitler rebuilt the air force anyway and boasted about its strength.

Lindbergh was eager to see the German planes because the Germans had become leaders in aviation technology in recent years. The Nazis, too, were eager to have Lindbergh see their developments. They believed that a positive report from him would increase the perception of Germany's military strength.

Charles and Anne Lindbergh flew to Germany in 1936, leaving Jon in the care of the Morrow family in New Jersey. In addition to visiting German airfields and aircraft manufacturers, the Lindberghs attended ceremonies given in Lindbergh's honor and met with many high-ranking officials in the German military. In the United States and England, however, many people were angered by Lindbergh's socializing with the Nazis because of the Nazis' anti-Semitic practices. Hitler blamed Germany's economic and social problems—extreme debt, inflation, and poverty—on the Jews. Under Hitler, the

Anne Lindbergh and son Jon pose with family pets at Long Barn, a cottage they rented near London.

Lindbergh (right) and his Nazi host inspect a German plane. The Nazis were eager to have the American aviator see their advancements in aviation technology.

Nazis had established the Nuremberg Laws, which denied Jews in Germany of their rights. The Nuremberg Laws made it illegal for Jews to marry ethnic Germans, vote, or hold public office. In addition, Jews were stripped of their German citizenship.

However, Lindbergh for the most part overlooked the Nazis' anti-Semitic practices. And at the end of his trip, Lindbergh had positive impressions of Germany and of Adolf Hitler. He wrote,

> I have come away with a feeling of great admiration for the German people. The condition of the country, and the appearance of the average person

whom I saw, leaves me with the impression that Hitler must have far more character and vision than I thought existed in the German leader who has been painted in so many different [negative] ways by the accounts in America and England.[64]

CONCERNS ABOUT WAR

Despite his admiration for the Germans, some of the things Lindbergh had seen during his visit concerned him. Seeing that country's buildup of military planes,

LINDBERGH AND DR. CARREL

One of the most influential figures in Charles Lindbergh's nonaviation life was his close friend and associate, Dr. Alexis Carrel. A Nobel Prize–winning French surgeon and scientist, Carrel's interest in the occult, mysticism, and genetic research made him a controversial figure in his field. Lindbergh, a self-taught amateur in science, met Carrel at the Rockefeller Institute in New York during the early 1930s. Under the doctor's tutelage, Lindbergh worked on a design for a mechanical pump that would keep blood circulating through a living organ. The notion especially appealed to Lindbergh because his sister-in-law, Elizabeth Morrow, suffered from heart disease; he hoped she could be saved by such a device. Lindbergh worked on the pump from 1930 to 1934, creating a working device that was the precursor of the modern artificial heart.

Lindbergh's association with Dr. Carrel became a source of media attention in the late 1930s because of Carrel's political and social ideas. Carrel was an admirer of fascist Italian dictator Benito Mussolini and, as biographer A. Scott Berg notes in his book *Lindbergh*, also espoused fascistic views:

> "[Carrel's] comments about civilization collapsing, modern nations saving themselves 'by developing the strong,' not 'by protecting the weak,' and his concern for the 'salvation of the white races,' sounded alarmingly like statements being uttered by [Nazi leader Adolf] Hitler."

Although Carrel opposed genocide and anti-Semitism, he did believe that the white race was genetically superior to all others. This view influenced Lindbergh's beliefs and helped shape the controversial speeches and articles Lindbergh delivered during the late 1930s and early 1940s.

for example, made him reconsider the nature of aviation. Before the trip he had thought of aviation as a means of bringing the world together. Afterward, he worried that it also had the power to tear the world apart. He wrote, "Cruising back to England after our visit, I found that Nazi Germany was forcing a reorientation of my thought. For many years aviation had seemed to me primarily a way of bringing the peoples of the world together in commerce and peace. . . . Now I began thinking about the vulnerability of men to aircraft carrying high-explosive bombs."[65]

In early 1937 this worry intensified. That year Lindbergh and Anne took a long trip to Asia, Africa, and Europe. When flying over Far and Middle Eastern countries, such as India and Egypt, he saw many once great civilizations in ruins. Centuries of warfare had destroyed them, and he feared that Western civilization could go the same way.

FRANCE

After his first trip to Germany in 1936, Lindbergh returned to England and saw his adopted country in a new light. After seeing the efficiency and the advanced technology of the Germans, he was dismayed that England, a country that had been a technological leader for more than one hundred years, had fallen so far behind.

Lindbergh's disenchantment with England and rising tensions between England and Germany also caused him to think about moving his family from England. Still not ready to return to the United States, the Lindberghs moved to France in summer 1938. They bought the islands of Illiec, off the northern coast, and moved into a house situated on the highest island. Charles Lindbergh loved living there. He enjoyed the wildness and the seclusion of the islands and spent a happy season in his new home with his family. The family included their third child, a son they named Land, born just before they left England.

In spite of the distractions and pleasures of the new home, Lindbergh's thoughts continually returned to his concerns about war. No matter what his family was doing, he wrote, "we felt the gusts of war."[66]

MINISTER LINDBERGH

In August 1938 Lindbergh traveled to the Soviet Union to gather information about that country's military aviation capabilities and to encourage diplomacy rather than military action among European countries. Although he was not allowed to view the Soviet air facilities, he was able to gather and to put together pieces of information from observation and interviews. He came away believing that the Soviet air force probably consisted of only several thousand planes and would be no match for Hitler's *Luftwaffe*. Further, Lindbergh came away with great apprehension about the Soviet system of government. He saw communism as a harsh and oppressive system. He wrote,

> My impression of Soviet aviation's mediocrity corresponded with my impression of the entire Soviet attempt at civilizing life, which was marked by millions of lives lost in the [1917 Communist] Revolution and in the liquidations [mass military executions] that followed, by the Siberian prison camps and the secret trials and executions, by the queues [lines] in front of stores and the scarceness of goods, by the fear of foreign contacts, by the control of information and the suppression of free speech. The Russians [Soviets] were a great people . . . [but] the system they lived under was destructive of life and incompatible with ideas of personal freedom so basic to the American mind.[67]

Vehemently anti-Communist, Lindbergh also began to believe that despite Hitler's anti-Semitic policies, a strong Germany served as an important barrier between the Soviet Union and western

Europe. "I was far from being in accord with the philosophy, policy, and actions of the Nazi government," he wrote, "but it seemed to me essential to France and England, and even to America, that Germany be maintained as a bulwark [barrier] against the Soviet Union."[68]

THE ALBATROSS

In October 1938 Charles and Anne Lindbergh visited Germany again. As had become customary, Lindbergh and his wife attended dinners with German govern-ment officials. One night Lindbergh dined without Anne at a gentlemen's dinner with several European diplomats and German dignitaries. During dinner Lindbergh discussed his and Anne's desire to move again. One of the guests encouraged Lindbergh to move to Berlin. Lindbergh considered it, thinking Berlin a very interesting city.

Also at the dinner was Air Marshall Hermann Göring, second in command only to Adolf Hitler. Göring presented Lindbergh with a military decoration for his services to the world of aviation. Lindbergh recalled his surprise at receiving the

Nazi Air Marshall Hermann Göring (right) shows Lindbergh a ceremonial sword.

medal. "When he [Göring] came to me he handed me [a] box and papers and spoke several sentences in German. I knew no German but I soon learned that he had presented me with the Order of the German Eagle, one of the highest decorations of the government."[69]

Later, when Lindbergh showed the medal to his wife, she called it the Albatross, a bird that symbolized doom in literature. She felt that the award, featuring the Nazi swastika and its accompanying parchment signed by Hitler, would be an honor that few would be happy about Lindbergh receiving.

OUTCRY AGAINST LINDBERGH

Two weeks after Lindbergh received the German medal, Nazi anti-Semitism turned violent. On the night of November 9, 1936, Nazi supporters attacked Jewish people and property throughout Germany and Austria. People were beaten and killed in the streets, and thousands of shops were vandalized. The night came to be called *Kristallnacht*—"night of broken glass"—and its barbarity and violence raised protest and outcry all over the world.

After *Kristallnacht* Lindbergh wrote in his journal that the Germans' treatment of the Jews puzzled him:

> I do not understand these riots on the part of the Germans. It seems so contrary to their sense of order and their intelligence in other ways. They have undoubtedly had a difficult Jewish problem, but why is it necessary to handle it so unreasonably? My admi-

ration for the Germans is constantly being dashed against some rock such as this. What is the object [goal] in this persecution of the Jews?[70]

Following *Kristallnacht* many in the press, American public, and U.S. government called Lindbergh a traitor for his friendly association with the Nazis and for his refusal to return his German medal. U.S. secretary of the interior Harold Ickes spoke out officially against Lindbergh, saying that anyone who accepted a decoration from Germany forfeited his right to be an American. Moviegoers booed images of Lindbergh when he appeared in newsreels, and his longtime employer TWA no longer called itself "The Lindbergh Line." Anne Lindbergh's reputation suffered also, as Jewish booksellers boycotted her latest book.

Although Charles and Anne Lindbergh were distressed by the outcry, Charles Lindbergh refused to return the German medal. He felt it would be an unnecessary insult to Germany and would damage his ability to act in a diplomatic capacity. However, when the Lindberghs did move again in 1938, they settled in Paris rather than Berlin. Lindbergh understood that a move to Berlin would be disastrous. "I do not wish to make a move that would seem to support the German action in regard to the Jews," he said.[71]

RETURNING TO AMERICA

Certain that a war in Europe was inevitable and German victory was certain, Lindbergh was determined to keep his native country out of the war. To do this, he felt that he had to return to the United States. Thus, in April 1939 the Lindberghs set sail to return to America. Once there, Charles Lindbergh hoped he could deter the U.S. government from going to war with Germany.

The same month, Hitler's armies invaded Czechoslovakia and in September 1939 invaded Poland. Following that invasion, Britain and France formally declared war on Germany. Initially, America sent no troops. The American president Franklin D. Roosevelt was an isolationist, but he also believed that the United States had to support the Allies in any way possible short of war. To this end, he sent money to Britain to support their war efforts and began developing legislation that would make possible more extensive support for Britain and France. Lindbergh, however, believed that it was a mistake for America to ally itself in such a way. He began to speak out on this view to the American public.

AGAINST THE TIDES OF WAR

In September 1939 Lindbergh wrote articles for the magazines *Atlantic Monthly* and *Reader's Digest* and broadcast a speech over the radio that criticized American intervention in the war. These articles and the speech were controversial for two reasons. First, the American government had already pledged its support to the Allies; to criticize the policy directly criticized the U.S. government. Second, the articles and speeches were obviously anti-Semitic and

revealed elements of racism in Lindbergh's character that the public had never seen. Lindbergh stated that the purpose of U.S. involvement in any war should be to protect the white race. He also argued that Asia, Africa, and the Soviet Union, not Germany, were the real threat to the white race. Further, in the *Reader's Digest* article entitled "Aviation, Geography, and Race," he said a strong Nazi Germany was necessary to defend the rest of Europe from Asia: "Only a western wall of race and arms can hold back the infiltration of inferior blood," he wrote, "and permit the white race to live at all in the pressing sea of yellow, black, and brown."[72]

PUBLIC AND PRIVATE CONTROVERSY

As the war in Europe escalated between 1939 and 1941, Lindbergh's articles and speeches became increasingly emphatic. Thus, while millions of Americans applauded his efforts to keep the country out of the war, many more began to regard him as a Nazi sympathizer, a traitor, and an anti-Semite.

After the Nazis captured France in 1940, Lindbergh delivered a speech saying that the fall of the rest of Europe to Germany was inevitable and that American intervention would be futile and foolhardy. For this speech, he received harsh criticism not only from the press and public but from the president himself. Roosevelt saw Lindbergh's isolationism as dangerous because he believed Lindbergh's popularity could convince many people

"Is Lindbergh a Nazi?"

During the late 1930s and early 1940s Charles Lindbergh's views on Germany and America's position on the war in Europe drew severe criticism. In 1941 a committee known as the Friends of Democracy published this letter to American citizens in a pamphlet called "Is Lindbergh a Nazi?" The pamphlet, filled with newspaper accounts and analysis of his articles and speeches accused Lindbergh of being a traitor, an anti-Semite, and a Nazi sympathizer.

"Dear Fellow American:

Charles Lindbergh is the great American tragedy. His spectacular Trans-Atlantic flight made him the world's best known aviator and his country's best loved hero. That was fourteen years ago. Today he is a hero only to the disciples of Adolf Hitler and to misinformed and misguided American isolationists.

But Lindbergh is more than a fallen idol. The flyer has turned politician, and his politics bear a strong resemblance to Nazism.

That is the tragedy of Lindbergh. It may be the tragedy of his country. . . .

Lindbergh has become a hero to all Nazis, both German and American. . . .[I]n his speeches and writings he has followed the Nazi propaganda line. Whether by coincidence or design, he has become the American voice of the Berlin Propaganda Ministry [a Nazi organization that produced anti-Semitic propaganda for Adolf Hitler].

This pamphlet uses Lindbergh's own words to show that he defends Nazi aggression while attacking Britain; that he believes in racism but not democracy; that he advocates a 'negotiated peace' with a man to whom treaties are mere scraps of paper. . . .

As the voice of the America First Committee, Lindbergh constitutes a very real threat to our democratic way of life. . . .

We present the evidence. Let the reader judge for himself."

to question American support of Britain and its allies. He called Lindbergh a defeatist, saying that he was too willing to see these countries give in to Hitler and Germany. Angry, Lindbergh resigned his decades-old commission as a colonel in the U.S. Army Air Reserve.

Many of Lindbergh's longtime associates and friends also broke off contact with him during this period. Anne Lindbergh's mother and sister, for example, publicly opposed his stance. And he began receiving hate mail. Lindbergh wrote,

Threatening letters are beginning to come in with the problems they always bring for us. . . . Of course, safety for my family lies in my keeping out of the public eye and the attention of the press. This is hard enough in normal times but in a period of crisis in which one's country may become involved in war, one must take part in the affairs of his country and exercise his influence in the direction he thinks right. I feel I must do this, even if we have to put an armed guard in the house.[73]

Lindbergh speaks at an America First rally. His membership in the controversial organization troubled many Americans.

AMERICA FIRST

The worst controversy for Lindbergh was still ahead of him, however. In March 1940, Lindbergh joined the America First Committee. This newly established but influential organization promoted American isolationism. Lindbergh's high profile established him as a speaker for the organization and he drew large audiences of people who opposed the war.

Lindbergh's affiliation with America First also drew negative attention. Although most of the members were opposed to war for moral or religious reasons, there were also a number of Communists and Nazi sympathizers affiliated with the group. Because of Lindbergh's affiliation with America First and his past actions and comments, President Roosevelt became convinced that Lindbergh was a Nazi sympathizer.

DES MOINES

In 1941 President Roosevelt enacted the Lend-Lease Act, a law that strengthened America's ability to support the Allies (Britain, France, and the Soviet Union) in Europe. Strongly opposed to this action, Lindbergh criticized the Roosevelt administration and the war in speaking engagements all over the country.

At an America First Committee meeting in Des Moines, Iowa, in fall 1941, he gave his most vehement and controversial speech. Entitled "Who Are the War Agitators?" the speech blamed the war on the British, the Roosevelt administration, and the Jews. In his speech, Lindbergh also pointed to what he called the negative Jewish influence over American media. He said, "Large Jewish ownership and influence in our motion pictures, our press, our radio, and our government constitute a great danger in our country."[74]

After delivering the speech Lindbergh was called a Nazi and a traitor by almost every newspaper in the country. The *San Francisco Chronicle* wrote, "The voice is Lindbergh, but the words are Hitler." And the *Des Moines Register* wrote that the

---

IN HER HUSBAND'S DEFENSE

Although Charles Lindbergh refused to respond to the media claims that he was anti-Semitic, his wife Anne Morrow Lindbergh wrote correspondence to friends, family, and business associates defending him. The following letter to a friend was published in her book War Within and Without: Diaries and Letters, 1939–1944.

"I want to say that if my husband were the man that the majority of the reading public of America today (as far as one can tell from the papers) thinks he is, I could not live with him. If he were what his words seem to many people to imply, I could not. . . . There is no hate in him, no desire to arouse hate. There is no plot or political scheming. . . . It is bitter for me to see him unctuously [smugly] condemned from the sidelines . . . by people who, if not anti-Semitic, at least fall into those obnoxious habits of speech and laughter that portray the hidden lines of superiority and inferiority in their own minds.

I have never heard my husband tell a Jewish joke. I have never heard him say anything derogatory about a Jew as such. . . . When he says he admires the Jews, he means it, and when he says he feels he is taking the one course that will prevent anti-Semitism in this country, he means it.

Anne Lindbergh strongly supported her husband and denied that he was anti-Semitic.

---

speech was "so intemperate, so unfair, so dangerous in its implications that it disqualifies Lindbergh from any pretensions of leadership."[75]

The American public also responded negatively to the speech. Feeling that Lindbergh had become an irrecoverable extremist and possibly a dangerous association, even prominent isolationists distanced themselves from him after the Des Moines speech. His actions angered so many that streets named in his honor after his 1927 flight were renamed, and the town of Little Falls painted over the words "Home of Charles Lindbergh" that had proudly emblazoned a water tower for more than a decade.

CLIPPED WINGS

Despite the negative response to his speech, in late 1941 Lindbergh prepared an even stronger one, planning to deliver it in mid-December. However, before he could do so, the Japanese, allies of Germany, bombed the American naval base at Pearl Harbor, Hawaii, on December 7 and drew the United States into the war.

Despite his isolationist views and his continued belief that the Germans would win, the attack on Pearl Harbor made Lindbergh realize that the United States had to respond. In his journal he wrote: "We have brought [war] on our own shoulders; but I can see nothing to do under these circumstances except to fight. If I had been in Congress, I certainly would have voted for the declaration of war. . . . Now that we are at war I want to con-

tribute as best I can to my country's war effort."[76]

Since Lindbergh had resigned from the army in 1940, he wrote to President Roosevelt to ask for reinstatement so that he could serve in the war. The president said he would return Lindbergh's commission if he agreed to publicly repudiate his isolationist views. Lindbergh, still convinced his views were right, refused. "It goes against my grain to be out of the Air Corps in time of war," he wrote, "but I am convinced it would be inadvisable for me to push my way back into it. . . . I am convinced that the stand I took on the war was right, and I believe this will be realized eventually."[77]

Lindbergh was angered and humiliated by the president's refusal to reinstate him. He decided, instead, to serve the country's war effort in the commercial sector. He would work as a consultant or test pilot for new war planes. But Roosevelt wanted to make it impossible for Lindbergh to work in aviation at all. "I'll clip that young man's wings,"[78] the president said. Roosevelt told aircraft companies that anyone who hired Lindbergh would not be awarded government contracts to build planes. Thus, Lindbergh was turned away by all of his longtime associates in the industry.

CIVILIAN CONSULTANT AND COMBAT PILOT

After several frustrating months of being refused work, in April 1942 an old acquaintance, car manufacturer Henry Ford, hired Lindbergh as a consultant at Ford's Willow Run, Michigan, factory

Lindbergh speaks with Henry Ford (left) at Ford's B-24 factory in Willow Run, Michigan.

where B-24 bombers were being produced. Ford and Lindbergh liked each other and had much in common. For one, they were the only two Americans to be awarded the German Eagle from Germany. Furthermore, both were isolationists, and both held anti-Semitic views. In addition, Ford was wealthy and powerful enough to do without government financial support; thus, Roosevelt's threats did not bother him.

That summer Lindbergh and his family moved to Detroit for his new job. The family now consisted of Charles, Anne, and four children: Jon, Land, Anne Spencer born in 1940, and Scott born in 1942.

Lindbergh worked very hard for the Ford plant. He worked most days from before dawn until nightfall, conducting test flights and developing ideas to improve the plant's efficiency. He was determined to prove himself an asset to the war effort. Although Ford said that he could have any salary he asked for, Lindbergh requested only $666.66 per month, the pay he would have earned as an Air Corps colonel.

A year later, the Roosevelt boycott of Lindbergh in the commercial industry eased. Roosevelt felt he had made his point and had other concerns to deal with. Lindbergh was hired as a consultant by an aircraft manufacturer called United Aircraft Corporation. There, he did many of the same jobs he had done for the Ford plant. But because his experience as a pilot was so extensive, he was also designated as a civilian observer. This allowed him to travel to the Pacific where the war with the Japanese was being fought. There he served as a flight instructor, sharing his knowledge about fuel conservation techniques with combat pilots.

Lindbergh also was allowed to conduct test flights of war planes in combat conditions. Recognizing that they had a skilled pilot and valuable combat asset in Lindbergh, the Marines unofficially encouraged him to engage in combat while on test and observation flights. Even though one Marine officer told him, "You have a right to observe combat as a technician but not to fire guns," another said with a wink, "Of course, it would be all right for him to engage in target practice on the way home."[79]

Thus, although it was against the rules, Lindbergh became an active war pilot. During his time in the Pacific he flew dozens of bombing and combat missions and shot down at least one enemy plane.

AFTER THE WAR

In May 1945 the war in Europe ended with the German surrender. (The war in the Pacific ended on September 2 when the Japanese surrendered.) Lindbergh returned to Germany for the first time

---

FROM ANOTHER TIME

Charles Lindbergh's youngest child, Reeve Lindbergh, was born in October 1945, after the end of World War II and after the controversy in the press regarding her father had faded. But, as she wrote in an article in Time *magazine in June 1999, while in college she discovered that the legacy of her father's prewar activities remained linked with his name.*

"I was virtually unaware of my father's prewar isolationism until I went to college and was shocked to learn that he was considered anti-Semitic. I had never thought of him this way. He never spoke with hatred or resentment against any groups or individuals, and in social discourse he was unfailingly courteous, compassionate, and fair. In the 1941 speech ['Who are the War Agitators?'], however, I could read a chilling distinction in his mind between Jews and other Americans. This was something I did not recognize in the father I knew, something I had been taught to condemn under the heading 'discrimination,' something from another time."

in five years. He was working as a consultant for United Aircraft Corporation studying German developments in high-speed aircraft. The destruction he saw as he and his coworkers flew into Germany dismayed him. The countryside and cities he had admired so much were in ruins.

In June Lindbergh traveled to the Bergen-Belsen concentration camp. Bergen-Belsen was just one of many such camps where the Nazis had murdered and cremated Jews by the millions throughout the war as part of Hitler's effort to rid the world of Jews. Although he found it disturbing, Lindbergh did not think that the concentration camps were much different from any other actions of war. "What the German did to the Jew," he said, "we are doing to the Jap [Japanese] in the Pacific."[80]

Many historians criticized Lindbergh's refusal to see the acts of the Nazis as more horrific than other aspects of war. However, as historian Arthur Schlesinger said, Lindbergh believed he was right, and eventually the controversy faded. "Lindbergh was a man of invincible confidence in his own rectitude and infallibility. He never wavered in the fact that he had been right. But he went on to other things and the world went on to other things."[81]

By the end of World War II, Lindbergh's public image had drastically changed from what it had been following his transatlantic flight eighteen years before. Although many people chose to forget his controversial words and actions leading up to the war, he was no longer America's hero.

Chapter

7 Descent

In the last three decades of his life Charles Lindbergh remained a busy and active man. But he preferred to remain largely out of the public eye. Doing so was easier after the war; his controversial prewar activities and views had alienated many of his fans and admirers. While the press never completely lost interest in Lindbergh, he was able to spend the last years of his life largely unbothered by the media. During these years he continued his work as an aviation consultant. He also became a prize-winning author and an active environmental conservationist.

NEW PURSUITS

After the war Lindbergh experienced some return of the popularity he had experienced prior to his controversial prewar activities. Some people now considered him a war hero because of his combat experience in the Pacific. And in recognition of his wartime activities, President Dwight D. Eisenhower reinstated Lindbergh's commission on April 7, 1954, awarding him the rank of brigadier general in the Air Corps.

Lindbergh also returned to work as a civilian consultant. He worked for the U.S. Air Force and Pan American Airways, providing technical advice and conducting test flights of new planes. As a consultant he traveled around the world many times.

But aviation, Lindbergh's first love, held less and less interest for him as time passed. Air travel had become increasingly commonplace in the years since the war. New planes were easier to fly. And Lindbergh thought the new technological advances like automated controls and instruments took the challenge out of flight. Although he never gave up flying, he spent his later years turning his mind and energies to other things, including his writing and the environment.

FAMILY

Following World War II, the Lindberghs bought a house in Darien, Connecticut, where they and their five children (the family now included their last child, Reeve, a daughter born in 1945) lived. Lindbergh was a loving but strict father. He played with his children and encouraged them to enjoy the outdoors as he had when he was a child. But he also

Lindbergh is photographed on a trip to the Philippines in 1970.

demanded their respect. He insisted they address him formally as "father," made them learn responsibility through chores, and spanked them when they misbehaved.

Lindbergh enjoyed his children, but his frequent traveling as a civilian consultant created distance between them and him. Thus as they grew into adulthood, he often tried to include them in his interests. For example in the late 1960s he invited his children and their spouses to visit him in Africa for a safari.

Lindbergh's frequent absences over the last decades of his life were also hard on his marriage. Anne Lindbergh often felt abandoned by her husband and several times considered leaving him. But she still loved him and, in spite of the frequent distance between them, repeatedly renewed her commitment to stay with him. Her children, her friends, and her writing provided her with refuge from the loneliness she felt.

The parents of five grown children by the 1960s, Charles and Anne Lindbergh bought a house on the eastern tip of the Hawaiian island of Maui. There, Anne continued her literary career, and Charles spent his last decades working on several volumes of memoirs, including his wartime journals, an autobiography, and *The Spirit of St. Louis*, a book begun in the late 1930s. He became a respected writer; *Spirit*, an account of his 1927 transatlantic flight, was completed in 1954 and won Lindbergh the Pulitzer Prize.

CONSERVATIONIST

Starting in the early 1960s Lindbergh also worked as a conservationist. He was concerned over the disappearance of the world's wildlife and wilderness. During his years of flying, Lindbergh worried about the vanishing American wilderness he saw from the air. He wrote:

In the decades I spent flying . . . I saw tremendous changes take place on the earth's surface. Trees disappeared from mountains and valleys. Erosion turned clear rivers yellow. Power lines and highways stretched out beyond horizons. . . . Almost everywhere I landed, I heard stories of disappearing wilderness, wildlife, and natural resources. Many species of animals that had taken epochs [millions of years] to evolve were, within decades, on the verge of extermination. I became so alarmed that I had to take some personal action.[82]

As a result, Lindbergh joined wildlife conservation groups, such as the World Wildlife Fund and the International Union for Conservation of Nature and Natural Resources. Lindbergh made significant contributions to conservation through these groups and on his own. For instance, in 1962, he flew around the world several times, cataloguing species of animals for the International Union. And, in 1964, he began writing articles on conservation.

LAST WISHES

Lindbergh's activism, travel, and other activities kept him busy until 1973 when he fell ill. He lost weight and could not stop coughing. Doctors diagnosed him with lymphoma, cancer of the lymph glands. He underwent radiation therapy for the cancer in January 1973. In an attempt to kill the cancerous cells, doctors exposed Lindbergh to high levels of radioactive waves, but this made him more sick. He lost thirty pounds and spent the next several months recuperating in Maui.

In early 1974 his health seemed to improve, and he made a trip to England to attend a fundraising event for the World Wildlife Fund. He also traveled to Connecticut and New York during the summer to visit friends and family. On that

MEDITATION ON DEATH

Charles Lindbergh concluded his last book, Autobiography of Values, *published posthumously in 1976, with these thoughts about mortality and death.*

"I grow aware of various forms of man and of myself. I am form and I am formless. I am life and I am matter, mortal and immortal. I am one and many—myself and humanity in flux. I extend a multiplicity of ways in experience and space. . . . My aging body transmits an ageless lifestream. Molecular and atomic replacement change life's composition. Molecules take part in structure and in training, countless trillions of them. After my death, the molecules of my being will return to the earth and the sky. They came from the stars. I am the stars."

trip, he felt ill again, and by July 1974 he was very weak. His doctors told him that his illness was terminal and that he did not have much longer to live.

Lindbergh accepted the diagnosis but wanted to go home, to Maui. His doctors advised against his making the trip because he was so weak, but Lindbergh was adamant and convinced them to let him go. Jon Lindbergh arranged to accompany his father on a commercial flight from New York to Hawaii; his mother, brother Scott, and sister Anne went also. During the flight, Charles Lindbergh lay in a bed, his family nearby to tend to his comfort.

After arriving in Maui on August 17, Lindbergh spent his last ten days carefully planning for his death. In these last days Anne and the Lindbergh children visited him and helped to take care of him. Lindbergh prepared his own funeral arrangements and even had his doctor fill out and sign his death certificate; the doctor left only the date blank to be filled in when Lindbergh died.

On the morning of August 26, 1974, Charles Lindbergh died, his children and his wife at his side. Per his wishes, Lindbergh was buried near their home in Maui to avoid the intrusion of the press.

LINDBERGH'S LEGACY

For most of his life, Charles Lindbergh was renowned for his 1927 transatlantic flight. His daughter Reeve Lindbergh remembers her father joking that no matter what he had accomplished in his life, people "still wanted to fly him off to Paris."[83]

Certainly Lindbergh's historic flight remains his primary legacy, but he is also remembered for his numerous contributions to aviation, science, and wilderness conservation. He pioneered commercial aviation, for instance, advancing the industry by obtaining money for and raising public interest in flight. He developed the prototype of the first artificial heart, and his work as an environmentalist raised consciousness, helped change legislation, and raised hundreds of thousands of dollars to preserve the world's wildlife.

Additionally, Lindbergh's legacy exists through the Charles and Anne Morrow Lindbergh Foundation, established by friends of the Lindberghs in 1977. The

Lindbergh was diagnosed with cancer in 1973. The great aviator died the following year with his family at his bedside.

THE NEW SPIRIT OF ST. LOUIS

In April 2002 Erik Lindbergh, Charles Lindbergh's grandson, replicated his grandfather's 1927 transcontinental and transatlantic flights in celebration of their seventy-fifth anniversary. Starting in San Diego, California, the thirty-seven-year-old woodworking artist and amateur pilot flew a plane dubbed the *New Spirit of St. Louis* across the United States to New York. Then he took off on April 20 for Paris.

Erik Lindbergh tried to stay as true to his grandfather's flight as possible, but some details of his flight were different. For example, although his grandfather took along only five sandwiches for sustenance on his thirty-three-and-half-hour voyage, Erik Lindbergh took six for his journey. Furthermore, the first flight took thirty-three-and-a-half hours, but the second took only seventeen. Speaking to Associated Press reporter Pamela Sampson, for an article entitled "Lindbergh's Grandson Lands in France," Erik Lindbergh said, "I did it in half the time and ate twice as much."

Charles Lindbergh's grandson, Erik, in 2002.

nonprofit organization works on projects related to Charles Lindbergh's interest in and concerns about science and the environment. The foundation provides grants and awards for individuals or groups whose work contributes toward the balance between technology and nature.

Finally, Lindbergh's legacy lives on in what he represented and continues to represent. For millions, he stood as an example of pioneering and adventure. Hundreds of books, websites, and articles are devoted to him. Each year thousands of people visit the sight of his boyhood home in Little Falls. His collection of medals and memorabilia are on display at the Lindbergh Museum in St. Louis, Missouri, and his plane, the *Spirit of St. Louis*, which still resides at the Smithsonian Institution in Washington, D.C., remains one of the Air and Space Museum's most popular exhibitions. It is clear that even though Lindbergh himself never understood the degree of admiration his achievements received, he remains an American icon and hero to millions of people.

Notes

Introduction: The Lindbergh Phenomenon

1. Fitzhugh Green, "A Little of What the World Thought of Lindbergh," from Charles Lindbergh, *We*. New York: G.P. Putnam's Sons, 1927, p. 236.

2. Quoted in PBS Video, *American Experience: Lindbergh*, 1990.

3. Reeve Lindbergh, "The Flyer: Charles Lindbergh: He Was the Century's First Hero and Unwittingly Pioneered the Age of Mass-Media Celebrity," *Time*, June 14, 1999.

Chapter 1: Fledgling

4. Charles Lindbergh, *Autobiography of Values*. New York: Harcourt Brace Jovanovich, 1976, p. 4.

5. Charles Lindbergh, *Boyhood on the Upper Mississippi: A Reminiscent Letter*. St. Paul: Minnesota Historical Society, 1972, p. 1.

6. Charles Lindbergh, *Boyhood on the Upper Mississippi*, p. 5.

7. Quoted in A. Scott Berg, *Lindbergh*. New York: Berkley Books, 1998, p. 42.

8. Charles Lindbergh, *Autobiography of Values*, p. 55.

9. Charles Lindbergh, *Autobiography of Values*, p. 7.

10. Charles Lindbergh, *Autobiography of Values*, p. 8.

11. Quoted in Berg, *Lindbergh*, p. 52.

12. Quoted in Berg, *Lindbergh*, p. 55.

13. Quoted in Zachary Kent, *Charles Lindbergh and the Spirit of St. Louis in American History*. Berkeley Heights, NJ: Enslow, 2001, p. 26.

14. Berg, *Lindbergh*, p. 63.

Chapter 2: Taking Flight

15. Berg, *Lindbergh*, p. 63.

16. Charles Lindbergh, *Autobiography of Values*, p. 9.

17. Charles Lindbergh, *We*, p. 41–42.

18. Charles Lindbergh, *We*, p. 43.

19. Charles Lindbergh, *Autobiography of Values*, p. 64.

20. Quoted in Leonard Mosley, *Lindbergh: A Biography*, Garden City, NY: Doubleday, 1976, p. 55.

21. Quoted in Berg, *Lindbergh* p. 74.

22. Charles Lindbergh, *Autobiography of Values*, p. 389.

23. Charles Lindbergh, *The Spirit of St. Louis*. New York: Charles Scribner's Sons, 1953, pp. 11, 15.

24. Charles Lindbergh, *The Spirit of St. Louis*, p. 12.

25. Charles Lindbergh, *The Spirit of St. Louis*, p. 15.

Chapter 3: Preparations

26. Quoted in Mosley, *Lindbergh, A Biography*, p. 125.

27. Charles Lindbergh, *The Spirit of St. Louis*, p. 85.

28. Quoted in Berg, *Lindbergh*, p. 100.

29. Charles Lindbergh, *The Spirit of St. Louis*, p. 119.

30. Charles Lindbergh, *The Spirit of St. Louis*, p. 130.

31. Quoted in Mosley, *Lindbergh: A Biography*, p. 132.

32. Charles Lindbergh, *The Spirit of St. Louis*, p. 131.

33. Berg, *Lindbergh*, p. 105.

34. Charles Lindbergh, *Autobiography of Values*, pp. 74, 75.

35. Charles Lindbergh, *Autobiography of Values*, p. 75.

36. Quoted in Barry Denenberg, *An American Hero: The True Story of Charles Lindbergh*. New York: Scholastic, 1996, p. 65.

37. Charles Lindbergh, *The Spirit of St. Louis*, pp. 184–85.

38. Charles Lindbergh, *The Spirit of St. Louis*, p. 185.

39. Quoted in Kent, *Charles Lindbergh*, p. 82.

Chapter 4: Fame

40. Charles Lindbergh, *Autobiography of Values*, p. 78.

41. Charles Lindbergh, *Spirit of St. Louis*, p. 354.

42. Charles Lindbergh, *Spirit of St. Louis*, p. 355.

43. Charles Lindbergh, *Autobiography of Values*, p. 78.

44. Quoted in Berg, *Lindbergh*, p. 124.

45. Quoted in Berg, *Lindbergh*, p. 125.

46. Quoted in Kent, *Charles Lindbergh*, p. 97.

47. Quoted in Berg, *Lindbergh*, p. 138.

48. Charles Lindbergh, *Autobiography of Values*, p. 80.

49. Charles Lindbergh, *Autobiography of Values*, p. 83.

50. Charles Lindbergh, *Autobiography of Values*, p. 118.

51. Anne Morrow Lindbergh, *Bring Me a Unicorn: Diaries and Letters of Anne Morrow Lindbergh, 1922–1928*. New York: Harcourt Brace Jovanovich, 1971, p. 195.

52. Anne Morrow Lindbergh, *Hour of Gold, Hour of Lead: Diaries and Letters of Anne Morrow Lindbergh, 1929–1932*. New York: Harcourt Brace Jovanovich, 1973.

Chapter 5: Tragedy and Danger

53. Quoted in Berg, *Lindbergh*, p. 227.

54. Anne Morrow Lindbergh, *Hour of Gold*, p. 202.

55. Charles Lindbergh, *Autobiography of Values*, p. 139.

56. Quoted in Berg, *Lindbergh*, p. 242.

57. Charles Lindbergh, *Autobiography of Values*, p. 139.

58. Anne Morrow Lindbergh, *Hour of Gold*, pp. 229, 230.

59. Quoted in PBS Video, *American Experience: Lindbergh*, 1990.

60. Quoted in Berg, *Lindbergh*, p. 274.

61. Charles Lindbergh, *Autobiography of Values*, p. 143.

62. Quoted in PBS Video, *American Experience: Lindbergh*, 1990.

63. Charles Lindbergh, *Autobiography of Values*, p. 144.

Chapter 6: Controversy

64. Quoted in Berg, *Lindbergh*, p. 361.

65. Charles Lindbergh, *Autobiography of Values*, p. 147.

66. Charles Lindbergh, *Autobiography of Values*, p. 162.

67. Charles Lindbergh, *Autobiography of Values*, p. 167.

68. Quoted in Berg, *Lindbergh*, p. 376.

69. Charles Lindbergh, *Autobiography of Values*, p. 181.

70. Charles Lindbergh, *The Wartime Journals of Charles Lindbergh*, New York: Harcourt Brace Jovanovich, 1970, p. 115.

71. Quoted in Berg, *Lindbergh* p. 380.

72. Quoted in PBS Video, *American Experience: Lindbergh*.

73. Charles Lindbergh, *Wartime Journals*, p. 282.

74. Quoted in PBS Video, *American Experience: Lindbergh.*

75. Quoted in PBS Video, *American Experience: Lindbergh.*

76. Charles Lindbergh, *Wartime Journals,* pp. 565, 566.

77. Charles Lindbergh, *Wartime Journals,* p. 584.

78. Quoted in Berg, *Lindbergh,* p. 437.

79. Quoted in Berg, *Lindbergh,* p. 449.

80. Quoted in PBS Video, *American Experience: Lindbergh,* 1990.

81. Quoted in PBS Video, *American Experience: Lindbergh,* 1990.

Chapter 7: Descent

82. Charles Lindbergh, *Autobiography of Values,* p. 32.

83. Quoted in PBS Video, *American Experience: Lindbergh.*

For Further Reading

Books

Zachary Kent, *Charles Lindbergh and the Spirit of St. Louis in American History.* Berkeley Heights, NJ: Enslow, 2001. Biography for young readers including excerpts from primary source material and good pictures.

Anne Morrow Lindbergh, *Listen! The Wind.* New York: Harcourt Brace, 1938. The story of Charles and Anne Lindbergh's survey flight around the North Atlantic Ocean in 1933.

———, *North to the Orient.* New York: Harcourt Brace Jovanovich, 1935. The narrative account of Charles and Anne Lindbergh's first exploratory voyage together.

Reeve Lindbergh, *Under a Wing: A Memoir.* New York: Simon & Schuster, 1998. Autobiographical memoir of Charles and Anne Lindbergh's youngest child.

Periodicals

Richard Cavendish, "Birth of Charles Lindbergh February 4th, 1902." *History Today*, February 2002.

Harry Miles Muheim, "My life with the Lone Eagle: The Trouble with Having (and Being) a Hero. (Visit to Pilot Charles Lindbergh's Grave)," *American Heritage*, May–June 1997.

People Weekly, "The Hero's Wife: Playing Second Lead in Her Husband's Storied Life, Anne Morrow Lindbergh Created a Compelling Role of Her," February 26, 2001.

Internet Sources

Charles and Anne Morrow Lindbergh Foundation, "Spirit of St. Louis 75th Anniversary," 2000. www.lindberghspirit.com.

Time, "*Time* 100 Heroes and Icons," 2002. www.time.com.

WGBH Educational Foundation, "Lindbergh, the American Experience," PBS, 1999. www.pbs.org.

Website

Charles and Anne Morrow Lindbergh Foundation Home Page (www.lindberghfoundation.org). Website advocating "a balance between nature and technology," with biographical information on Lindbergh and Anne Morrow Lindbergh, a photo gallery, timeline of aviation history, and other features including a list of places named after or in honor of Lindbergh.

Video

Public Broadcasting System, *The American Experience: Lindbergh*, 1990. Excellent biographical documentary including original source footage, interviews with Lindbergh family members, and commentaries by Lindbergh historians, critics, and authors.

Works Consulted

Books

A. Scott Berg, *Lindbergh*. New York: Berkley Books, 1998. Pulitzer Prize–winning, in-depth biography of Charles Lindbergh including extensive histories of his ancestors as well as of Anne Morrow Lindbergh and her ancestors.

Barry Denenberg, *An American Hero: The True Story of Charles Lindbergh*. New York: Scholastic, 1996. Juvenile biography of Charles Lindbergh's entire life with extensive quotations and numerous black and white photographs.

Zachary Kent, *Charles Lindbergh and the Spirit of St. Louis in American History*. Berkeley Heights, NJ: Enslow, 2001. Biography for young readers including excerpts from primary source material and good pictures.

Anne Morrow Lindbergh, *Bring Me a Unicorn: Diaries and Letters, 1922–1928*. New York: Harcourt Brace Jovanovich, 1971. The letters and diaries of Charles Lindbergh's wife, Anne Morrow Lindbergh, covering the years up to her meeting and marriage to Lindbergh.

———, *The Flower and the Nettle: Diaries and Letters, 1936–1939*. New York: Harcourt Brace Jovanovich, 1976. The letters and diaries of Charles Lindbergh's wife, Anne Morrow Lindbergh, covering the years leading up to World War II.

———, *Hour of Gold, Hour of Lead: Diaries and Letters of Annie Morrow Lindbergh, 1929–1932*. New York: Harcourt Brace Jovanovich, 1973. The letters and diaries of Charles Lindbergh's wife, Anne Morrow Lindbergh, covering the years leading up to the kidnap and murder of their son.

———, *Locked Rooms and Open Doors: Diaries and Letters, 1933–1935*. New York: Harcourt Brace Jovanovich, 1974. The letters and diaries of Charles Lindbergh's wife, Anne Morrow Lindbergh, covering the years following the kidnap and murder of their son.

———, *War Within and Without: Diaries and Letters, 1939–1944*. New York: Harcourt Brace Jovanovich, 1980. The recollections of Charles Lindbergh's wife, Anne Morrow Lindbergh, in the years leading up to and during World War II.

———, *The Wave of the Future: A Confession of Faith*. New York: Harcourt Brace, 1940. Anne Morrow Lindbergh's essay, written as the United States became drawn into World War II.

Charles Lindbergh, *Autobiography of Values*. New York: Harcourt Brace Jovanovich, 1976. Lindbergh's autobiography focusing on the years leading up to and during World War II.

———, *Boyhood on the Upper Mississippi: A Reminiscent Letter.* St. Paul: Minnesota Historical Society, 1972. A long essay written by Lindbergh about his childhood on the family farm near Little Falls, Minnesota. Excellent pictures and original source material.

———, *The Spirit of St. Louis.* New York: Charles Scribner's & Sons, 1953. Written in the years following World War II, this autobiography details Lindbergh's life from his days as a U.S. Air Mail pilot in the late 1920s to his world famous transatlantic flight. This book won the Pulitzer Prize in 1953.

———, *The Wartime Journals of Charles Lindbergh.* New York: Harcourt Brace Jovanovich, 1970. The diaries of Charles Lindbergh, kept during the years leading up to and during World War II, the only time of his life when he kept extensive journals of this kind.

———, *We.* New York: G.P. Putnam's Sons, 1927. Lindbergh's first book, describing the story of his life, his transatlantic flight, and his views on aviation.

Leonard Mosley, *Lindbergh, A Biography.* Garden City, NY: Dell, 1976. Very good biography of Lindbergh written three years after his death.

Periodicals

Reeve Lindbergh, "Charles Lindbergh: He Was the Century's First Hero and Unwittingly Pioneered the Age of Mass-Media Celebrity," *Time,* June 14, 1999.

Julia Richards, "We Saw Him Land!" *Smithsonian,* May 2002.

Index

Picture Credits

Cover: © Bettmann/CORBIS

© AP Photo/Tom Gannam, 99

© Associated Press/AP, 66, 96

© Bettmann/CORBIS, 29, 32, 53, 59, 73, 79, 82, 85, 89, 90, 92

© Frank Scott Clark/Minnesota Historical Society, 17

© CORBIS, 26

Jeff DiMatteo, 45, 47, 55

© Hulton/Archive by Getty Images, 11, 41, 43, 56, 61, 64, 68, 71

© Monroe P. Killy/Minnesota Historical Society, 50

© Mareau/Minnesota Historical Society, 22

© Minnesota Historical Society, 14, 19, 21, 27, 34, 38, 76, 81, 98

© Nelson/Minnesota Historical Society, 16

© Smithsonian Institution, 48

© Swenson Studio/Minnesota Historical Society, 37

About the Author

Andy Koopmans is the author of three books, including *The Importance of Bruce Lee* and *Madonna*. He lives in Seattle, Washington, with his wife Angela Mihm, dog Zachary, and cats Bubz and Licorice. He is the grand-nephew of John van der Linde, the chief mechanic at Ryan Aircraft who turned the propeller on Lindbergh's *Spirit of St. Louis* for its first test flight in San Diego, California, in 1927.